The Van Hoven Heritage

Norma Alkema

© 2025 Norma Alkema

The cover shows an embroidery piece that my sister, Barb Schild, made as a gift for my parents, Jack and Mildred Van Hoven.

All rights reserved. No part of this book may be used or reproduced in any manner without written permission.

This book is in honor of my father, Jacob "Jack" Van Hoven.

Preface

Family history has always fascinated me. In 2019 I published *The Life and Legacy of Smith Cook*. My mother's maiden name was Cook, and the book's subject was her great-grandfather. *The Van Hoven Heritage* is an account of the family history of my father, Jacob "Jack" Van Hoven.

When the family gathered for birthdays and holidays, Dad was a great storyteller. These accounts may have been about his own childhood or about one of our relatives that we didn't really know. Dad told us about working at his Uncle Mart's farm every summer, starting when he was eight years old until he was 18. He would share how much his uncle did for his family, saying "You know, Uncle Mart and Aunt Fanny did not have children, so they always had young relatives helping at the farm. Uncle Mart knew that my brother, Richard, needed surgery on his legs because he'd had polio, and he paid for the surgery so Richard could walk." Dad also told the story about his grandfather's encounter with Native Americans out West. I loved all those stories so I was compelled to collect my parents' histories for this book. My parents and I would get together regularly, and I began taping our conversations about their stories so I wouldn't miss anything.

As I began to gather information about my father's ancestors, I found that most of them had left their homes in the Netherlands for a better life in the United States, specifically in Grand Rapids, Holland, and Zeeland, Michigan. Some came looking for work and for a better way to take care of their families. Some came for the freedom of worshipping God as they felt called. Because they loved their families, they supported each other however they could. They raised strong families who were good and faithful workers and set an example of sacrificing for those they loved. Out of gratitude and a sense of responsibility, they contributed in many ways to their new homeland, and to the communities in which they lived. Their love for God was evident in their family lives, and they shared their faith with others.

My Van Hoven ancestors' many sacrifices made life difficult at times, but we, their descendants, benefitted greatly. Many of them left great examples for us to follow, and I will be forever grateful.

Lovingly researched by Norma Alkema, 2025

Psalm 16: 5-6: The Lord is the portion of mine inheritance and of my cup: thou maintainest my lot.
The lines are fallen unto me in pleasant places; yea, I have a goodly heritage.

Contents

Chapter 1	The Van Hoven Ancestors	1
Chapter 2	The Haan and Pos Families	7
Chapter 3	Jacob and Irene (Wentzel) Van Hoven	17
Chapter 4	Gertrude Dena (Van Loo) Van Hoven's Paternal Ancestry	23
Chapter 5	Gertrude Dena (Van Loo) Van Hoven's Maternal Ancestry	35
Chapter 6	The Melle and Tryntje (Westerbeek) Vanden Bosch Story	43
Chapter 7	The Story of Henry and Gertrude Dena (Van Loo) Van Hoven	49
Chapter 8	The Story of Jack and Mildred (Cook) Van Hoven	65
Chapter 9	Jack and Mildred Van Hoven's Children Have Families of Their Own	87
Chapter 10	Van Hoven Events Through the Years: 1966-1983	99
Chapter 11	A New Generation and Many Goodbyes	111

CHAPTER 1
The Van Hoven Ancestors

THE VAN HOVEN side of the family comes from Ouddorp, a village in the municipality of Goedereede in the province of Zuid-Holland (South Holland), the Netherlands. I can trace my DNA back eight generations, mostly from Ouddorp, before my ancestors came to the United States. Some members of the Van Hoven family still live in Ouddorp today.

The meaning of Ouddorp is "old village." Ouddorp is still a picturesque, charming and old-fashioned town.
Image courtesy Wikimedia Commons

Ouddorp started as a Roman settlement and underwent many developments over the centuries. These developments were influenced by the village's proximity to the sea and by the interventions of its citizens. One example of this is *impoldering*, which means that wetlands are turned into *polders* (land that is reclaimed from the sea) by building dykes around it. Since the twelfth century, polders have characterized the Netherlands.

For a long time, elements that were yielded from the land and sea formed the most important source of income for the people of Ouddorp. Agriculture was small-scale, and included the cultivation of chicory, which was used to produce red dye and substitute coffee. Traces of this cultivation are still visible in the Ouddorp landscape. The men who worked for fisheries made a profit from the local waters by using flat bottom boats to catch mainly shrimps. Many of the old picturesque houses and farms remain scattered in Ouddorp. The lives and work culture of Ouddorp residents were influenced by long-standing traditions and modern changes.

The village of Ouddorp itself was designed in a circular pattern around the *Dorpskerk* (town church). This church, originally Roman Catholic, was built in the Middle Ages. Records indicate that, in 1348, the church had a free-standing tower, and also a church choir. The church became part of the Dutch Reformed denomination in the late 1800s and was dedicated to Saint-Maarten, who is said to protect beggars and geese. In 1903, conference rooms were added between the church and the tower. The structure was damaged in 1944 during World War II and restored in 1946-47.

South of Ouddorp is a *terp*, or artificial hill, on which Spreeuwenberg Castle was built in the 13th century, but today only the hill remains. To provide power, the De Hoop grist mill was built in

1845, and was restored between 1882-1884. A lighthouse was built in Ouddorp in 1911; German soldiers destroyed the original lighthouse during World War II, on May 4, 1945, and Lighthouse Westhoofd was built as a replacement in the late 1940s, and it still stands.

The Zuiderzee, a bay in the Netherlands. Old land is pictured in green, with the new land (polders) in darker green.
Image courtesy Wikimedia Commons

The town church of Ouddorp, pictured in 2009, is now part of the Restored Reformed Church denomination.
Image courtesy Wikimedia Commons

Ouddorp was home to 1,951 people in 1840. In 1850, a harbor was constructed to the south of the village. Because much of the land around Ouddorp was farmland, the harbor was used to transport farm goods to other areas. Ouddorp's 11-mile beach is the longest in the Netherlands. After World War II, the beach started to develop as a seaside resort. In 2013 Ouddorp became part of the municipality of Goeree-Overflakkee.

In my research, the first Van Hoven ancestor that I could find was **Joannes Hove** (1673-1696). Joannes was born in Wouderberg (in the province of Utreckt, the Netherlands), and he also died there. He married **Jantje Wulferts de Bruijn**, also born from Wouderberg, and she died there in 1701. Joannes and Jantje Hove are my 7th great-grandparents.

Johannes and Jantje Hove's son, **Frans Jansz Van Hoven** (1693-1749) may have been born in Wouderberg, but he primarily lived in Ouddorp, where he married **Susanna Arens Lauwe** (1697-1766). It is not known why an "n" was added to the Van Hove surname. Frans and Susanna Van Hoven are my 6th great-grandparents.

Frans and Susanna Van Hoven had two girls and one boy. That boy was **Jan Fransz Van Hoven** (1723-1796), who married **Cornelia Beeuwsier** (1726-?). They are my 5th great-grandparents, and they lived in Ouddorp.

Jan and Cornelia Van Hoven had 4 girls and 5 boys. One of their sons, **Aren Van Hoven** (1756-1817), married **Adriaantje Koert** (1766-1835), who was born in Schlipruthen, Olpe, Nordrhein Westfalen, Germany. Adriaantje's family can be traced back four generations in Germany, all the way back to 1655, where her 2nd great-grandfather **Georg Hoppe** (1655-1708), my 8th great-grandfather, was born. Jan and Cornelia Van Hoven are my 4th great-grandparents.

Aren and Adriaantje's only child was their son, **Jan Arense "John" Van Hoven** (1788-1852). He married **Kreintje Ruit** (1793-1847) in Ouddorp. Jan and Krientje Van Hoven are my 3rd great-grandparents, and they had four girls and two boys: Aren Jansz (b. 1811), Maartje J. (b. 1815), Araantje Janse (b. 1818), Baaltje Jo (b. 1822), **Abram Jansz** (b. 1826), and Cornelia (b. 1829).

Abram Jansz Van Hoven (1826-1892), my 2nd great-grandfather, was born and raised in Ouddorp. He married **Trientje Vogel** in 1846, and their daughter, Tryntje "Catherine" Van Hoven was born on December 24, 1847.

Painting of a windmill on a polder "In the Month of July" by Paul Joseph Constantine, 1889
Image courtesy Wikimedia Commons

Abram and some other relatives had begun talking about moving to the United States. We don't know why for sure, but we do know that the Netherlands, like many other European countries, suffered from serious crop failures such as the potato blight (1845-1849), also referred to as the "Hungry Forties." The blight resulted in great poverty, hunger, and disease. Dutch immigration to America increased again following the European Revolutions of 1848, when peasants demonstrated against terrible conditions. The failure of the Dutch revolutionists led to a small wave of political refugees, who fled to America.

Most Dutch immigrants who came to Michigan settled in rural areas such as Holland and Zeeland. This group, also called Seceders, came to America for religious reasons. They had a strong commitment to church life and to the purity of Calvinistic doctrine, and wanted to keep the Reformed heritage free from state domination. The Seceders also had a deep desire to have a closer, more personal relationship with God; they formed close relationships with fellow churchgoers, with small groups meeting for worship. Worship, and the expression of their faith, were important to Seceders, but Dutch rulers forbade church meetings that exceeded twenty people, so they were fined heavily and frequently imprisoned. Many were ejected from their farms; their businesses were boycotted and they were socially ostracized.

The first group of Seceders came to West Michigan late in 1846, arriving in Holland, Michigan in early 1847. The total number of settlers in the Holland/Zeeland area in 1847 was 457 persons. The first town building was a church. The town of Zeeland was platted in 1849, and the school district was organized the following year.

In 1953 the Holland colony had 4,000 inhabitants. However, rural life became intolerable for many Dutch immigrants, and the hardships drove them to bigger, more established cities. As one relative told it, "Of the sufferings, privations, and struggles of these early settlers no one not familiar with pioneer life can form any conception. Locating in a dense wilderness without means, without roads, unacquainted with the language or institutions of the country, inexperienced in the severe toil required to clear up heavy timber land, suffering from diseases incident to the living around the swamps and to process of acclimation. Many gave up the struggle and moved to Grand Rapids, Kalamazoo, Grand Haven, and other places, some to return again when better days dawned. The majority, however, were 'stayers.' "

Abram Van Hoven had a brother, Aren, who was 15 years older than Abram. Aren and his wife, Klassje Molesteeg, decided to make America their new home, along with other relatives: Abram's sister Baaltje Jo (who was 4 years older than Abram) and her husband, Klaas Langstraat, and Abram's sister Cornelia Janse (who was two years younger than Abram) and her husband, Johannes Packaart. We do not know when most of them came, but we do know that Baaltje and Klaas, Aren and Klassje, and Abram and Trientje settled in or near Paris, Kent County, Michigan. We also know that Abram's sister Cornelia and her husband Johannes Packaart arrived at Ellis Island on August 16, 1852, and settled in Paterson, New Jersey.

Passenger list: Household heads, and independent persons

VAN HOVEN, ABRAM

Trienty (Vogel) Van Hoven — wife
Kryntje Van Hoven — daughter

Code:

Age	1	24
Sex	1	Male
Women	1	1
Children	1	1
Occ (occupation)	11	Workman
Rel (religion)	1	Dutch Reformed CH.
Cls (Econ class)	2	Less well to do
Asm (assessed tax)	2	No
Resn (reason)	3	—
Yr (year)	49	1849
Prov	11	Beijerland, Zuid
Mun (municipality)	93	Oudorp

I believe that the other Van Hoven families were already in Michigan by 1852. I have narrowed down the timeframe for Abram and Trientje's arrival the best that I could. Their daughter, Tryntje "Catherine," was born on Dec. 24, 1847 in Ouddorp, the Netherlands, so their arrival in the United States could not have been earlier than 1848. I believe that they may have arrived in 1849, as the stories that are told indicate that they came with a toddler. Just recently, I read some material that my second cousin in California shared with me. It says that Abram and Trientje Van Hoven, his first wife, arrived in the year 1849, when Abram was 24 years old. Then I found the following immigration record from the ship manifest, which contains typographical errors that were common during immigrations at that time:

After I studied the material even more, I came to believe that Aren and his family traveled on the same ship. Abram's sister, Baaltje Jo, and her husband, Klaas Langstraat, may also have come on that ship.

Things did not go well for the Abram Van Hoven family when they settled in the Grand Rapids area, and great sorrow came Abram's way. After the long trip to a new land, Trientje became very ill, and before long she passed away. Abram was left with a little daughter who needed her mother, and he felt that he needed a wife, too.

Typical Friesian Head-Neck-Body Farmhouse
The "head" in front is the residence; the "neck" in the middle is the kitchen, and the "body' is the barn.
Image courtesy Wikipedia Commons

Sketch depicting Dutch immigration to America, 1840s
Image courtesy Wikimedia Commons

CHAPTER 2
The Haan and Pos Families

MY THIRD GREAT-GRANDPARENTS are **Gijsbert Haan** (1801-1874) and **Marritje Pos Haan** (1800-1876).

Gijsbert's family, the Haans, can be traced back eight generations to the city of Hilversum, which is in the province of North Holland, the Netherlands. Marritje Pos's family can be traced back ten generations to the village of Oud-Loosdrecht, located in the town of Loosdrecht-Utrecht. Oud-Loosdrecht, which is about 15 miles from Hilversum. Gijsbert and Marritje Haan were said to have had thirteen children, only ten of whom survived.

Haan and Pos Families Heritage

Haan	Pos
My 4th Great-Grandparents:	
Peter Haan & Tymtje Rykse Das	Gijsbert Klaasz Pos & Magteldje Land
1750-1822 1774-1812	1768-1827 1768-1827
My 5th Great-Grandparents:	
Gijsbert Haan & Aagje Haan	Klaas Jacob Pos & Marrietje Soetbrood
1725-1765 1726-1765	1736-1806 1740-1808
My 6th Great-Grandparents:	
Matthijs Gerritsz Haan & Gijsbertje Vlaanderen	Jacob Harmensz Pos & Wijntje Jansd Groen
1697-1778 1700-1798	1696-1781 1700-1752
My 7th Great-Grandparents:	
Gerrit Klaassen Haan & Aaltje Mathijsz Fabri	Harmen Jacobsz Pos & Grietje Teunisd Meijers
1672-1742 1677-?	1663-1701 1668-1728
My 8th Great-Grandparents:	
Klaas Haan	Jacob Jacobsz Pos & Geertje Harmens
1647-?	1639-1684 1668-?
My 9th Great-Grandparents:	
	Barend Jacobsz Pos & Jannette Peters Vlaming
	1605-1660 1605-1667
My 10th Great-Grandparents:	
	Jacob Hart Pos & Barbara Sibilla Paulise
	1560-? 1575-?

Interior of a farm near Hilversum
(a 19th-century drawing by Johannes Bosboom)
Image courtesy Wikimedia Commons

19th-century postcard, Hilversum
Image courtesy Wikimedia Commons

Rev. Albertus van Raalte

At this time, people in the Netherlands were facing social and religious persecution, as well as severe famine and diseases, so many citizens were considering emigration to the United States of America. in 1836, Alburtus van Raalte, a Dutch minister, visited Michigan's Lower Peninsula, where a man encouraged him to settle in the Holland area. Van Raalte found the area amenable for farming; farmers in the Netherlands paid high taxes and had very little land, so van Raalte sent a handbill to his home country that described this beautiful area with fertile soil. Farmers immigrated in droves, and van Raalte became the spiritual leader for the newly established colony.

It was February 9, 1847 when a small group of settlers led by Rev. Albertus C. Van Raalte built its first cabins nearly three months after the group's ship, "The Southerner," reached the New World in November of 1846.

The Haan family sailed on *The Centurion,* which landed in New York on July 26, 1847. From there, they traveled to Holland, Michigan, where they settled. Dutch immigrants tended to be hard-working, and besides farming, they were willing to explore new types of jobs to improve their livelihood. There is evidence that many Dutch immigrants became prosperous, and their property values rose steadily. In 1855 a Holland Township farm, together with cattle and tools, sold for about $3,000, which would be about $110,000 in 2025. In Zeeland Township, a smaller farm of 56 acres (of which 12 had been cleared) went for $775, which would be equivalent of over $2,000 today. Crops flourished and the harvests were abundant. In the middle of August, the corn stood 9 feet tall.

Also during this time, new threshing machines were coming into use in the settlement. An editor of *De Hollander*, a local publication, reported that people believed that progress was being made on all sides, "as every person can see with his own eyes. All the Dutch population was at work and growing richer every day." Two years later, Zeeland Township had grown to 259 families. Horses and mules numbered 48 and pigs were now 873.

The Centurion
Image courtesy Wikimedia Commons

Dutch immigrants who were farmers found the land in West Michigan to be suitable for agriculture.
Image courtesy Adobe Stock

Gijsbert Haan was a pastor, and he quickly became well-known. The Haan family had aligned themselves with the Reformed Church in America (RCA). Pastors in the area made up a classis, which was a governing body, for their churches, and most were happy with the RCA rules. But Pastor Haan found the RCA inadequate. Over time, largely due to the dissension that was expressed in Pastor Haan's preaching, talk began to grow, and others began to feel that the RCA was theologically lax. When Pastor Haan wrote to the classis with documents of secession, some of the arguments were that the RCA conducted "open communion," sang hymns whose lyrics were not based on Biblical psalms, and overlooked catechism preaching.

Although the classis did not approve of the secession, one church did leave the RCA in January of 1857. It was not long before other churches followed suit. In 1859, these secessionist churches became the True Dutch Reformed Church. More name changes took place until 1904, when the church adopted its present name, the Christian Reformed Church (CRC).

The first church in Zeeland, built in 1848 and made of logs, was often called the prettiest of the first churches. It was made of square cedar logs and had a little tower on the top with a bell. The ringing of the bell was a familiar sound as it was rung twice on Sundays to call people to worship. It was also rung to call the community to meetings and rang vigorously to worn of fire danger. It was rung slowly when there was a death, sadly tolling the number of years of the person's life. The church grew so rapidly in its first year that a larger church had to be built.

Pastor Gijsbert Haan

Marritje Pos Haan

In June 1849 the Zeeland Church had 175 families, 225 members. Zeeland had a Dutch school at which teachers gave instruction in Catechism and Psalm singing as well as in reading and writing. Financial income was small. People had been poor, and what little they had went to purchase land. In 1878, the Christian Reformed Church built a brick house of worship on Main Street in Zeeland.

The second church in Zeeland, Michigan, was made of logs, as was the first church.
Image courtesy Wikimedia Commons

Christian Reformed Church
Zeeland, Michigan
Image courtesy Wikimedia Commons

It can be said of Gijsbert Haan that he was a man of strong faith and that he served the Lord faithfully all his life. He preached from God's Word in the Dutch Christian Reformed Church for many years, and he died in 1876 at the age of 74. Marritje also died in 1876, at the age of 75. They are both buried at Fuller St. Cemetery, Grand Rapids, Michigan.

Gijsbert and Marritje Haan's ten children lived to adulthood and had families of their own:

1. Tymetje Haan (1820-1901) married Gijsbert Grootveld, a carpenter. They lived in Grand Rapids until Gijsbert died in 1874. They had six children. Some time after Gijsbert's death, Tymetje moved to Chicago, Illinois, where she later died.

2. **Magdalena Haan** (1821-1889) married **Abram Van Hoven** (1826-1892). (See below for more details.)

3. Gysbert Haan (1824-1869) married Christina Van Der Slik, and they made their home in Holland, Ottawa County, Michigan. They had six children.

4. Peter Haan (1830-1896) married Catherine Rankins, and they farmed in Coopersville, Ottawa County, Michigan. They had seven children.

5. Nicholas Haan (1832-1914) married Annegtje Hendriks, and they farmed first in Zeeland but later lived in Wayland, Allegan Country, Michigan. They had seven children.

6. Marretje Haan (1834-1881) married Aart Van Sledright. They lived in Paris, Kent County,

Michigan, and Art was a farmer. They had six children.

7. Wyntje Haan (1836-1879) married Marinus "Martin" Witters. They lived in Grand Rapids, 3rd Ward, where Martin worked as a carpenter. They had five children.

8. Tyme "Timothy" Haan (1839-1887) married Cornelia "Nellie" VerDer Slik, and they lived in Grand Rapids, Ward #1. Timothy was a chair maker. They had four children.

9. Jacob Haan (1841-1899) married Catherine Van Hoven on May 17, 1866. (see page 16)

10. Aagie Anje Haan (1846-1920) married William Vander Hull. Records indicate that Aagie married a couple other men also over the years. She had no children.

The Marriage of Magdalena Haan and Abram Van Hoven

The marriage of **Magdalena Haan**, Gijsbert and Marritje's second daughter, is of note because she married **Abram Van Hoven**, my second great-grandfather. You will recall, from Chapter 1, that shortly after Abram, Trientje, and Catherine Van Hoven settled in the Grand Rapids area, Trientje became ill and quickly passed away, leaving behind her husband and daughter.

Gijsbert Haan, besides being a pastor, was a skilled carpet maker. It so happened that Abram Haan was also a carpet maker, and the two men met. Abram got to know Gijsbert and Marritje's daughter, Magdalena, who was a couple of years older than he. Magdalena had a lot of experience caring for children, as she had helped her mother in the family's busy household. Abram and Magdalena were married on January 5, 1852. The photo of their wedding was damaged at some point. The minister who officiated at Abram and Magdalena Van Hoven's wedding wrote the following:

Abram and Magdalena Van Hoven, circa 1852

January 5, 1852 were married by me:

Abram Van Hooven age 27 years and Magdalena Haan age 29 years in the presence of Frans Van Driele and Gerrit Dalmen, all live in Kent County, Michigan.

(Signed) C vd Meulen,
Minister of the Gospel

Through this marriage, Abram now had a wife and Catherine had a mother; Magdalena also became my second great-grandmother. The small Van Hoven family settled down in Wyoming, Kent County, Michigan. Abram worked hard, weaving carpets on a big loom in his home, before becoming a farmer.

Abram became a citizen of the United States in 1855. It was not long before the family began to grow. Abram and Magdalena had seven children; see below for details of their lives.

Early postcard, Dutch family on the docks of Black Lake, later called Lake Makatawa
Image courtesy Wikimedia Commons

By 1860, Abram and Magdalena and family were living in Paris, Grand Rapids, Kent County, Michigan, and Abram was listed as a farmer in the census that year. They belonged to the Second Central Reformed Church in Grand Rapids at that time. The story is told that Abram went to church very, very early, well before the rest of the family. He always stood on a kitchen chair to put on his Sunday pants so they would not get dirty. People thought that he had a rather ugly disposition.

By 1870, Zeeland Township had acquired a sawmill, a wagon factory, blacksmith shops, grocery stores and a post office. The 1870 census shows that the Abram and Magdalena Van Hoven family lived in the Zeeland/Holland area. Abram had his own farm, and his personal estate was valued at $300; his real estate was valued at $2,000. They joined the Vriesland Christian Reformed Church while living in the area.

Magdalena died in 1889 at the age of 68, and Abram died in 1892 at the age of 66. They were buried in Vriesland Cemetery, Zeeland, Ottawa County. Their seven children grew up and had families of their own:

1. **Marritje "Mary" Van Hoven** (1852-1929) married John Fox, and they had 6 children. They lived in Zeeland, Michigan all of their lives. As a young husband and father, John sold sewing machines. When he was 49, he went totally blind; he died at the age of 72. Mary lived to be 77. They were both buried in the Zeeland Cemetery.
2. **Jan "John" Van Hoven** (1855-1941) married Kaatje "Catherine" Ver Hage. John was a farmer in Jamestown, Michigan, and he and Catherine had 7 children. John died at the age of 86 and was buried in the Jamestown Cemetery.
3. **Gysbert "Gilbert" Van Hoven** (1856-1950) married Rietje "Nellie" Wyngarden, and they settled in Zeeland, where they would live for their entire lives. Gilbert and Nellie became farmers, and later Gilbert worked as a string butcher. The couple had 9 children, one son and eight daughters. Rietje died at the age of 52 and Gilbert lived to be 94; they were buried in

Zeeland Cemetery.

4. **Cornelia Van Hoven** (1858-1947) married Heinerick Faber in 1877, and they had 6 children. Heinerick was a farmer, and he died in 1917 at the age of 64. Cornelia lived to be 89; they were both buried in Zeeland Cemetery.

5. **Jacob Van Hoven** (1861-1945) was my great-grandfather. He married **Reintje "Irene" Wentzel** (1863-1939) (see their story in Chapter 3)

6. **Arend "Arie" Van Hoven** (1863-1947), loved music as a child. The love of music in the Van Hoven family was probably due to Magdalena's influence. Arie made a fiddle for himself, which he loved to play. Father Abram must have been just as rigid in his beliefs about music as was his father-in-law, Gijsbert Haan. When Abram found out about the fiddle he was outraged, and he called it "devil possessed." Abram took it from Arie, smashed it, and threw it out.

    Arie and Reka (Berghorst) Van Hoven

    Arie left home in 1897 at the age of 16 and moved to Beaverdam, where he worked at a sawmill. While there, he met Reka Berghorst, the oldest of the 13 children of Sabas and Gristje (Kok) Berghorst. Arie and Reka, both 18, were married on October 14, 1881, at Arie's parents' home in Grand Rapids, Michigan. The young couple settled in Vriesland, Ottawa County, Michigan, and became farmers.

    Arie and Reka Van Hoven had 3 children. They named their first daughter after Arie's mother, Magdalena, and they called her Maggie. Daughter Sena was born four years later, and Abraham (Abie), who was named after Arie's father, was born about six years after Sena.

    Arie was a great hunter and marksman, so he provided his family with a lot of meat. Besides farming, Arie worked in a sawmill, as a carpenter, and as a well digger during his short life. One day when Maggie was 10 years old, her father announced that the family was moving to Zeeland. Arie built a house for the family on Harrison Avenue; he built four more houses in Zeeland, and it is interesting to note that those houses, now remodeled, are still in use today.

    A great tragedy came to the family when the children were young. On May 25, 1895, while Arie was cleaning his gun, the gun went off, sending a bullet to his brain. After a couple days of deep suffering, Arie Van Hoven died at the age of 32. Thus, Reka Berghorst Van Hoven became a widow at the age of 31; it was up to her to raise Maggie (12), Sena (8) and Abie (18 months old). Tragedy struck again when Sena died at the age of 12. Reka died in 1938 at the age of 74.

7. **Aagje "Agnes" Van Hoven** (1867-1916) married Jacob Bos in Zeeland on Nov. 12, 1890. They had 8 children, 7 of whom lived to adulthood. Soon after 1900 they moved to Los Angles, California, where Jacob worked as a blacksmith. When Agnes died at the age of 49, she was

buried back home in Zeeland Cemetery. Jacob and most of the family continued to live in California, where Jacob died in 1952 at the age of 85.

Left to right: Virginia, father Jacob Bos, John, mother Agnes with Gertrude and Jerry in front of her, Magdalena, Arther G., and Violet

Jacob and Agnes (Van Hoven) Bos

The Marriage of Jacob Haan to Catherine Van Hoven

As noted above, the marriage of **Magdalena Haan** (Gijsbert and Marritje Haan's daughter) to **Abram Van Hoven** was quite significant in my family's history. Another marriage of note was that of Magdalena's youngest brother, **Jacob Haan** (ninth child of Gijsbert and Marritje's Haan) to **Catherine Van Hoven**. An even greater bond was created between the Haan and Van Hoven families through this union because Catherine was the daughter of Magdalena's husband, Abram Van Hoven, by his first wife, Trientje. I wonder what it was like for Magdalena to be both aunt and grandmother to Jacob and Catherine's children.

Jacob was a carpet weaver, like his father. He was a Civil War veteran, having served from 1863-1865 in the 1st Michigan Engineers. After they were married, Jacob and Catherine lived in Grand Rapids, Michigan. They had 12 children, of which 5 died prematurely.

The Jacob and Catherine (Van Hoven) Haan family

Back row, left to right: sons Peter (1879-1948), Gilbert, (1867-1938) and Abram (1877-1929)
Middle row: sons Nicholas (1884-1960) and John (1881-1957)
Front row: Jacob (father), daughter Tunie (1868-1883), son Jacob (1890-1959) and Catherine Van Hoven Haan (mother)

Children missing from picture who had already passed away: daughter Tunna (1868-1883), daughter Mary (1870-1886), and three little girls named Magdalena, all who lived less than a year: Magdalene 1 (1883)

Grand Rapids, Michigan attracted many immigrants because of the commercial benefits that were available because of its waterways. The original Pearl Street bridge was built in 1858 for $16,000.
Image courtesy Wikimedia Commons

CHAPTER 3
Jacob and Irene (Wentzel) Van Hoven

MY GREAT-GRANDFATHER, **Jacob Van Hoven** (1861-1945), was Abram and Magdalena Van Hoven's 5th child. He grew up on the family farm, which was about three miles east of Zeeland. **Jacob** married **Reintje "Irene" Wentzel** (1863-1939), my great-grandmother, on December 1, 1880, at the First Reformed Church of Zeeland, where they were members. Rev. Steffens officiated at the ceremony. Jacob was 19 and Irene was 17. In the previous chapter, you have read about Jacob Van Hoven's lineage. I will now focus on his wife, my great-grandmother Irene's heritage.

Jacob Van Hoven   Irene (Wentzel) Van Hoven

The Wentzels, Irene (Wentzel) Van Hoven's Paternal Ancestry

- **Irene's** parents, my 2nd great-grandparents, were **Johannes Hendrick Wentzel** (1828-1913) and **Agatha Sneller** (1832-1910); they lived in the village of Olderbroek, in the the province of Gelderland, the Netherlands.
- My 3rd great-grandparents were **Hendrick Johannes Wentzel** (1798-1869) & **Aarttje Dijkman** (1798-1876), also from Olderbroek.
- My 4th great-grandparents were **Johann Henrich Wentzel** (1755-1838) & **Johanna Geurts** (1762-1846), also from Olderbroek.
- My 5th great-grandparents were **Heinrick Wentzel** (1715-?) & **Johanna Heun** (?), from Frielingen, Hersfeld, Hesse-Naasau, Prussia, Germany
- My 6th great-grandparents were **Johan Heinich Wentzel** (1685-1741) & **Agnes Weignand** (?), who lived in Berlin, Germany.
- My 7th great-grandparents were **Johan Heinich Wentzel** & **Anna Christine Gundelack**

Irene Wentzel's mother, Agatha Wentzel, died in 1910 at the age of 78 and her father, Johannes Hendrick Wentzel, died in 1913 in Holland, Michigan, at the age of 85. Agatha and Johannes were both buried in the Zeeland Cemetery.

Johannes and Agatha (Sneller) Wentzel and Magdalena (Haan) Van Hoven and Abram Van Hoven

Jacob and Irene (Wentzel) Van Hoven

Agatha and Hendrick were both buried in the Zeeland Cemetery.

Many Dutch emigrants, more than 100,000 in the 1800s, often came from poor, rural areas. It was not easy to scrape together the cost of ship fares, and people often had to sell their meager possessions. It was difficult to leave all that they knew behind, but they had hopes for a better life.
Image Courtesy Wikimedia Commons

The Snellers, Irene (Wentzel) Van Hoven's Maternal Ancestry

As mentioned previously, **Irene's** parents, my 2nd great-grandparents, were **Johannes Hendrick Wentzel & Agatha Sneller.** Irene's father's heritage was presented previously, and now I will tell you about her mother Agatha's side, the Snellers.

• Agatha's parents were **Jan Reijersz Sneller** (1787-1871) and **Reyntje Mol Sneller** (1791-1882); they were my 3rd great-grandparents, and they lived in Oldebroek, in the province of Gelderland, the Netherlands.

• My 4th great-grandparents were **Reijersz Gerritsg Sneller** ((1737-1813) & **Rijkje Hendricks Flier** (1744-1817), also from Oldebroek.

• My 5th great-grandparents were **Gerrit Reijersz Sneller** (1697-1775) and **Hendrika Lubberts** (1701-1776), also from Oldebroek.

• My 6th great-grandparents were **Reyner Claasz Ruler** (1650-?) and **Bijgkien Goosens** (1965-?), also from Oldebroek.

• My 7th great-grandparents were **Claasz Geertsen Reijers** (1619-?) and **Marriskjen van de Denekamp** (1621-?), also from Oedenbroek.

• My 8th great-grandfather was **Geertsen Reijers** (1603-?), from the Netherlands.

The Jacob and Irene (Wentzel) Van Hoven Family

Standing in back row, left to right: Alice, Gilbert, Abram, Leonard and Agatha

Seated, left to right: Father Jacob Van Hoven, John "Henry" (my grandfather), Marion, Mother Irene (Wentzel) Van Hoven, and Katherine

Irene grew up on the Wentzel family homestead, which was about one mile east of Zeeland. The hill on which it was located was then known as "Wentzel Hill." Later, when the highway was built, the Wentzel homestead was torn down. Irene worked as a domestic before her marriage, and she also worked in her aunt Mrs. Fox's millenary store.

After their marriage, Jacob bought a farm a half-mile north of Beaverdam Crossing. After he had farmed for several years, the family moved to Zeeland. When Zeeland was a village, he was on the board of trustees and an alderman. He was also a member of the hand-pumping fire department for fifteen years. In 1892 Jacob started a farm implement business called Van Hoven and De Pree on East Main St. in Zeeland, where he worked until 1911. From that point on, his business was called Van Hoven and Verekee, and he worked there until 1934. At the age of 74, he worked in his son Gilbert's retail store as a salesman. Jacob and Irene Van Hoven had nine children. (See following page for more details.)

Jacob had a very serious, sometimes harsh personality, but Irene was a gentle and loving person. Jacob may have inherited some of his father's stern disposition, but he did not share any of his father's religious fervor or beliefs. The Van Hovens did not attend church often, according to their grandson, my father Jacob "Jack" Van Hoven. Jack also remembers his grandfather as "someone you couldn't get close to." One of Jacob and Irene Van Hoven's children only lived until the age of 2, but the other 8 children lived to adulthood and had families of their own:

1. **Abram Van Hoven** (1882-1952) married **Kate Vanden Bosch** on October 4, 1906. She was the daughter of Gerald Vanden Bosch and Maria Van Ecklenburg. Abram and Kate lived in Grand Rapids and they had no children. During his lifetime, Abram was a painter, decorator, and custodian. I remember that Uncle Abe used to join our family when we visited Grandma and Grandpa Van Hoven. He always had something for any child who came in the door. I received a lot of pretty little hankies from him. My favorite was a Little Boy Blue hankie, which I still have. If he did not have something special, he would always give us money. He died in 1952 at the age of 70. Aunt Kate died in 1966 at the age of 82. They were buried in Zeeland Cemetery.

Abram and Kate (Vanden Bosch) Van Hoven

2. **John "Henry" Van Hoven** (1884-1970) was my grandfather, and he married **Gertrude Dena Van Loo** (1888-1952) in 1907. Their story is told in Chapter 7.

3. **Leonard Van Hoven** (1886-1971): As a young man, Leonard worked as a clerk in Lansing, Michigan, at the state capital. On February 21, 1911, he married **Gladys Bookwalter** in Dighton, Osceola, Michigan. They later lived in Zeeland. Leonard first worked as a bookkeeper for an engine company, and later he was a proprietor for the sale of farm implements. He ended his career as a bookkeeper for a wholesale lumber company. Leonard and Gladys had three children: Jean, Leonard Jay and Virginia. Gladys died on April 9, 1964

at the age of 71, and Leonard died on May 27, 1971 at the age of 85. They were buried at Zeeland Cemetery.

John "Henry" Van Hoven   **Leonard Van Hoven**

4. **Agnes Van Hoven** (1888-1976) married **James Timmer**. Their first home was in Zeeland, then they moved to Grand Rapids where James was a building contractor in construction. They had 2 daughters, Ruth and Shirley. James died in an accident while working in Marion County, Indiana, on June 22, 1951 at the age of 58. Agnes died on May 14, 1976 in Grand Rapids, Michigan, at the age of 88. Both were buried at Rest Lawn Memorial Park in Grand Rapids.

Aunt Agnes

5. **Katherine "Katie" Van Hoven** (1891-1970): At the age of 19, Katie worked at the cigar company, as did many other Dutch immigrants and their children. It was grueling work to hand-strip the sturdy stem from tobacco leaves, and the employees worked in sweltering heat.

Katie married **Benjamin Nyson** in 1916 in Zeeland. Benjamin was a merchant in a grocery store in Zeeland. They had one son, Robert Nyson. By 1930 the family were living in Grand Rapids, where Benjamin also worked as a merchant in a grocery store. Within ten years, Benjamin was promoted to branch manager for retail groceries. He died in 1968 at the age of 75, and Katie died at the age of 79 in 1970. They were buried in Zeeland Cemetery.

6. Gysbert (born on 1/9/1894), sadly died before he was two years old on September 24, 1894.

7. **Gilbert J. Van Hoven** (1896-1972) loved photography. After attending business college in Lansing, he worked at the Zeeland State Bank. He was in the U.S. Navy, where he served as Yeoman, third class for the State of Michigan during World War I, from June 5, 1918 to March 4, 1919. He stayed stateside because he was very ill when his unit shipped out.

Gilbert married **Mamie Johanna Derks** on Oct. 2, 1919. He worked as a bookkeeper for a company that sold farm machinery and implements. By 1930 he was the proprietor of a similar company. Gilbert and Mamie had a daughter, Doris J., and a son, Ronald Glenn. By 1940 Gilbert was the co-owner of a hardware and farm equipment store. The family lived all their lives in Zeeland. Gilbert died in 1972 at the age of 76, and Mamie died in 1978 at the age of 77. They were buried in the Zeeland Cemetery.

Gilbert and Mamie Johanna (Derks) Van Hoven

8. **Alice Van Hoven** (1898-1990) lived at home with her parents until she was 47 years old, when she married **Cornelius Dekker**, who was a 63-year-old widower on June 1, 1946. Cornelius, a baker with the Rusk Factory, had a grown daughter from his first marriage. After Alice and Cornelius had been married for just three years, he died in 1949 and was buried in Pilgrim Home Cemetery. Alice died in 1990 at the age of 91 and was buried in Zeeland Cemetery.

9. **Marian "Mary" Van Hoven** (1906-1968) married **John Bergsma** on October 11, 1927, in Grand Rapids. They had two sons, Ned J. and Roger Jack. John was a finish sprayer in a furniture company. In 1939, Marian and John were divorced. Marian and the boys moved to Zeeland, where she found work as a typist. She died in 1968 at the age of 62 was buried in Zeeland Cemetery.

Most of these aunts and uncles attended the Dutch Christian Reformed Church in Zeeland, at least as children.

CHAPTER 4
Gertrude Dena (Van Loo) Van Hoven's Paternal Ancestry

AS MENTIONED IN CHAPTER 3, my grandfather, **John "Henry" Van Hoven** (1884-1970) married my grandmother, **Gertrude Dena Van Loo** (1888-1952) on March 7, 1907 in Zeeland. You have read about Henry Van Hoven's background in the previous chapter, and in this chapter I will present my grandmother **Gertrude Dena Van Loo's** ancestry.

Gertrude Dena was the daughter of **Dirk Van Loo** (1846-1923) and **Grietje "Gertrude" Vanden Bosch** (1848-1899), who were my great-grandparents. On the following pages I will provide details of Gertrude Dena's paternal ancestors, the Van Loo family.

In 1949, **Dirk Van Loo** (my great-grandfather) emigrated to the United States with the rest of his family when he was 3 years old. His parents were **Willem Van Loo** (1814-1873) and **Maria (Ver Poorte) Van Loo** (1813-1879), and they were my 2nd great-grandparents. Willem's parents, **Willem Van Loo** (1790-1864) and **Janna de Waard** (1789-?), were my 3rd great grandparents. Willem's parents were **Willem Van Loo** (born before 1770) and **Barbara Visser** (born before 1770-?), and they were my 4th great grandparents. They all died in Nisse, Netherlands.

The Van Loo family members were among the 216 Hollanders who came to the Dutch settlement in 1849. In 1847, the family had received an offer from the well-to-do Dutchman, Jannes Van de Luyster, who offered to pay the Van Loos' passage to America. Willem, even though he was a Seceder, did not feel like emigrating in 1847; one reason was that he had plenty of work as a carpenter. Two years later, a 51-year-old Dutch peddler by the name of Jan Samallegange, made the offer again to take them, but again Willem was hesitant until Maria convinced him otherwise.

As their son, Cornelius, told it, "Father hesitated, but mother, who was a bright woman and considered the future of the children, convinced father. This is the way we arrived in this good land, like many other, kindly assisted by Samallegange."

Their ship, the *De Louvre*, probably left Rotterdam early in March, 1849, arriving at New York on May 4, 1849. The immigrants left New York in a canal, going up the Hudson River and Erie Canal, then to Buffalo. From there, they took the Great Lakes steamers to Detroit, and via Milwaukee to Grand Haven, where some of them took the Grand River Scow to Grandville. The Van Loos loaded their belongings in a wagon drown by two oxen and followed an Indian trail to the Dutch settlement, arriving at the colony on May 26, 1849.

Jan Samallegange was also a passenger on the *De Louvre*. He had become a well-to-do farmer in the province of Zeeland, the Netherlands. He brought several needy families that had been in his employ in the Netherlands, (including the William Van Loo family), to the Dutch colony in West

Michigan. Sadly, a few weeks after his arrival he died while returning from a trip to Chicago. He was buried on the shifting sand dunes on the north side of and near the mouth of the Kalamazoo River. Among the families he sponsored was the Van Loo family.

It appears that Willem was an avid church attender, although he seemed to change churches often. He is listed as a member of the First Reformed Church of Zeeland at the time the family lived briefly in Montcalm County in 1950. At the time of the Secession movement, 15 families in Zeeland left the Reformed Church and began the First Christian Reformed Church of Zeeland. Willem Van Loo was a signer of one document of one of the new churches. The True Reformed Church was organized some time between 1858 and 1862. Dirk, Willem, and Maria Van Loo were all listed as members there.

The Willem and Marie Van Loo Family

Back row: Cornelius, Dirk, Gertrude
Front row: Janna, father Willem, mother Marie
(not pictured: son Willem and daughter Lydia)

Willem was a farmer in the Zeeland area. The Native Americans in the Holland/Zeeland area were friendly, peaceful, and helpful. They taught the first Zeeland settlers the skills of wilderness living; the snaring and hunting of wild game and in particular the unaccustomed work of felling trees as Zeeland was founded in the depths of a forest of tall pine, monster oaks, and cedars. Everyone needed to clear land for farming and build homes. Willem and Maria's children were as follows:

1. **Willem "William" Van Loo** (1836-1838) was 13 when the Van Loo family emigrated to America. He married a woman named Marie, and they lived in Big Rapids, Michigan. William worked as a merchant in 1870. They had two children; Willie C. (b. 1866) and Kingsby (b. 1869).
2. **Cornelius Van Loo** (1838-1927) was 11 when the family emigrated; when he grew up he married Jannetje "Kate" Van Loo. Cornelius and Kate's story is told below.
3. **Lydia Van Loo** (1840-1849) was 9 when the family emigrated, but she died soon after the family settled in Zeeland. She was buried in Zeeland Cemetery.
4. **Gurtruida "Gertrude" Van Loo** (1842-1918) was 7 years old when the family emigrated; as an adult she married **Tamme Vanden Bosch**. The story of the Vanden Bosch family is told in Chapter 6.
5. **Jan Van Loo** (1844-1845) lived for about a year. He died in Driewegen, the Netherlands.
6. **Dirk Van Loo** (1846-1923) arrived in the United States when he was 3 years old. When he

grew up he married **Grietje "Gertrude" Varden Bosch** (1848-1899), and they were my great-grandparents. Gertrude's parents, my 2nd great-grandparents, were **Melle Vanden Bosch** and **Tryntje Westerbeek Vanden Bosch**.

7. **Janna "Jane" Van Loo** (1849-1902) was the only Van Loo from Willem's family to be born in the United States. She was born in Buffalo, New York (in Erie County), before the Van Loo family moved to Michigan. Jane married Matthew Rozema, who had immigrated to the U.S. from Germany in 1867. Matthew was a farmer in the Zeeland area. Jane and Matthew had ten children. In 1900 the family was living on a farm in Allendale, Michigan. Jane died there in 1902 when she was 53 years old, and Matthew died in 1928. Both were buried in the Zeeland Cemetery.

On the following pages, I will provide further details of two of Willem and Maria (Van Poorte) Van Loo's children. Cornelius and my great-grandfather **Dirk**, were very close even though Cornelius was eight years older than Dirk. They were both strong men who were mightily used by God. They were also very different, as you will see from their stories.

Cornelius Van Loo, my 2nd great-uncle

Cornelius was born on August 7, 1838, in Driewegen, the Netherlands and emigrated at the age of 11. Cornelius attended Michigan Agricultural College in Lansing from 1858-1859 and then he attended Albion College and Seminary for two semesters, from 1859-1860. From 1860-1861, he taught school in Montcalm County.

All too soon, the Civil War began, and on August 15, 1861, 24-year-old Cornelius enlisted in Ionia, Michigan. He joined the 21st Regiment, Michigan Infantry, Company F as a Corporal with Colonel William B. McCreery. After the Battle of Stone River in Murfreesboro, Tennessee, in January 1863, he became First Lieutenant Cornelius Van Loo. He commanded his company for 20 months.

In February 1863, a young man named Chauncy H. Peck wrote a letter to his family from the battlefield: *"I'm unwell at present. Cornelius Van Loo has been in command of the Co. since the fight. He is a very smart fellow. Many soldiers are being discharged from the service. I think there are not but a few who would like to get discharged if they could. A great many officers have resigned. All seem too tired of war except our speculating generals."*

On September 20, 1863, Cornelius was twice wounded in action at Chickamauga, Georgia, but he refused to leave his unit. An exhibit at The Dekker Huis Zeeland Museum mentioned the following about Cornelius: *"Although severely wounded in the leg, where an enemy bullet lodged and remained with him till death, he refused to leave his company, but with great discomfort keep his place in the ranks."*

Cornelius Van Loo

21st Regiment, Michigan Infantry, Company F

It was Cornelius's privilege to cast his first ballot for President Abraham Lincoln in 1864 on the battlefields of Georgia. During his military career, he would march all the way to the Atlantic Ocean coast in Savannah, Georgia, with Sherman. He was mustered out of the service and honorably discharged on June 8, 1865, in Washington D.C. After the war, Cornelius returned to Albion College to continue his education.

On August 24, 1867, Cornelius married Jannetje "Kate" Van Loo, whose parents were Josia Van Loo and Cornelia Ver Merris Van Loo. Cornelius and Kate lived in Grand Haven, Michigan, where Cornelius became a farmer. He was a Republican and spent much of his life in public service:

- 1869-1875: elected three times as Register of Deeds in Ottawa County, In 1875 the family moved from Grand Haven back to their farm in Zeeland, which was a mile south of the Mead Johnson and Company factory.
- 1881-1883: represented Ottawa County in the Michigan House of Representatives. He farmed in Zeeland for seven years then sold the place in 1883 and moved into the city of Zeeland.
- 1883-1901: devoted his life to the real estate business with Martin Elzinga. They helped at least 30 families procure farms in the Borculo area.
- Served as Superintendent of Schools for four years, and Supervisor and Chairman of the County Board of Supervisors for two years.
- 1890: organized, along with other men, the Zeeland Furniture Manufacturing Company. He was elected secretary and treasurer of the company, and held those offices for the entirety of the company's existence, which was more than 36 years.
- April 18, 1895: elected President (Mayor) of Zeeland

Early Pioneers of the Village of Zeeland
Fortieth anniversary celebration of the settlement of Zeeland, August 31, 1887
Note: Cornelius Van Loo is #3; Melle Vanden Bosch is #18

Cornelius and Kate Van Loo had 12 children; only three of the girls lived to adulthood. They also adopted one boy, Benjamin Cornelius, whose name before the adoption was Uitermark.

Marie	1869	lived 2 ½ months
Willem J.	1871	lived 1 ½ months
Mattie I.	1871	lived 3 months
John R.	1872	lived 29 days
Mary Rebecca	1872-1886	lived 14 years
Cornelia	1875-1876	lived 4 months
Benjamin Cornelius	1872-1943	
Jozias	1877	lived 6 months
Cornelia	1878-1965	(Mrs. William Glerus)
Willie	1880-1881	lived 10 months
Gertrude	1881-1969	(Mrs. Edwin Glerus)
Rosalie	1883-1949	(Mrs. Henry VanDyke)
Willie	1887	lived 23 days

How my heart goes out to Cornelius, but especially to his dear wife, Kate, who carried so many children but lost seven little babies. Another child lived to be 14.

When the League of Nations was formed on June 28, 1919, Cornelius said, *"The League of Nations is a 'sign of the times' and in my opinion is the forerunner of the dawning of the 'millenneal age', giving up advance information of the time when the God of heaven shall set up a kingdom which shall never be destroyed..."*

Zeeland became a very well-to-do town. On August 31, 1887, a celebration was held to commemorate the settlement's Fortieth Anniversary.

Cornelius also wrote poetry (courtesy of Zeeland Historical Society):

```
Reminiscence and Desire, by C. Van Loo, 1919

        At five could read, and speculate
        On strong desire to emigrate.
        But now, I'm growing old!

        At ten by boyish wish I got,
        And left with youthful joy the spot
        Where stood my home and childhood's cot.
        But now, I'm growing old!

        I jumped a fence, I was so spry,
        And when I walked the dust did fly,
        Stunts many I could do, but my,
        I now, am growing old!

        As soldier I marched to the sea
        None better on the tramp could be,
        I lived on sweet potatoes, see
        But now, I'm growing old!

        In legislating took my share,
        And in debate was always there
        Nor shrank from duty anywhere.
        But now, I'm growing old!

        I long for rest, but now behold
        Around me battles manifold
        To beat the League, or we are sold
        And now, alas, I'm growing old!

    Come back, O twentieth spring!  Renew
    My strength as 'twas before I knew
    Of League or Wilson or his crew.
        But now, I'm growing old!

        Oh could I gird me on once more
        To help the nation, threaten'd sore,
        Shout for it's rescue as of yore.
        But now, alas!  I'm old, I'm old!
```

Another poem by Cornelius:

```
When ma is sick                    When pa is sick
  She pegs away;                     He's scared to death
She's quiet though                 An' Ma an' us
  Not much to say                    Just hold our breath
She goes right on                  He crawls in bed
  A-doing things                     An' puffs and grunts,
An' sometimes laughs               And does all kinds
  Er even sings.                     Of crazy stunts.
She says she don't                 He wants "Doc" Brown
  Feel extra well                    An 'mighty quick.'
But then it's just                 For when Pa's ill
  A kind 'o-spell                    He's awful sick
She'll be all right                He gasps and groans
  Tomorrow sure.                     An' sort o' sighs.
A good old sleep                   He talks so queer,
  Will be the cure.                  An' rolls his eyes.
An' Pa he sniffs                   Ma jumps an' runs,
  An' makes no kicks                 An' all of us.
For women folks                    An' all the house
  Is always sick.                    Is in a fuss.
An' Ma she smiles                  An' peace and joy
  Lets on she's glad -               Is mighty skeerce -
When Ma is sick                    When Pa is sick
  It ain't so bad.                         It's something fierce.
```

By C. Van Loo, 1890

Cornelius's wife, Kate, died at the age of 78 and Cornelius died in 1927 at the age of 89 after a 9-month illness. They were both buried in Zeeland Cemetery. The following was written after Cornelius's death in one of the Zeeland papers:

"When Mr. Van Loo came to this country at the age of ten years, he found this section a vast unbroken forest, and beset by wild animals of every kind native to this state and by a savage people that outnumbered the immigrants. From this state of things he has seen it grow into the beautiful prosperous country it now is, with its cities, its towns, its farms, and its factories. He has tasted the bitterest poverty with its corn bread and water, and its brush shanties, and he has tasted the prosperity that was lavishly spread by the hand of plenty. He has given of his in support of others when he was poor, barely able to get along and he has given of his when giving meant no sacrifice. Of his alms none or few ever knew, although they were not lacking, and his love for the helpless and children was manifest. The good he has been for Zeeland will never be appreciated, but its fruits will live on for our benefit. Zeeland loses much in the demise of Cornelius Van Loo."

Cornelius in later life

Dirk Van Loo, my great-grandfather

Dirk Van Loo married **Grietje "Gertrude" Vanden Bosch** (1848-1899), and they were my great-grandparents. Gertrude was the daughter of **Melle Vanden Bosch** (1819-1897) and **Tryntje Westerbeek Vanden Bosch** (1820-1902). **Melle** and **Tryntje Vanden Bosch** were my 2nd great-grandparents, and the Vanden Bosch's story is told in Chapters 5 and 6.

After they were married, Dirk and Gertrude settled in the Zeeland area, where Dirk became a farmer and gardener. Later in life he also became a carpenter, and he worked in that trade for many years. On February 21, 1899, Dirk's wife Gertrude died at the age of 51. The story has been told that she died in a house fire, but her death certificate lists *La-grippe* (which is the French word for influenza) as the cause of death. La-grippe was often called the Spanish flu. Dirk and Gertrude had 6 children:

1. **Willem** (1867-1943) became a banker. In 1886 he married Dena Krokkee, whose parents were Adrian Krokkee and Cornelia Willemse. They had 5 children: Gertrude (b. 1886), Cora (b. 1892), Dora Mae (b. 1898), Maurice (b. 1902) and Chester Earl (b. 1909). Dena died at the age of 71 on May 25, 1939 and William died at the age of 76 on Nov. 29, 1943. They had lived in Zeeland all their lives and were buried in Zeeland Cemetery.

Willem Van Loo

**Wedding Photo
Martin and Fanny Van Loo**

2. **Marinus "Martin" "Mart"** (1869-1938) Van Loo was Dirk and Gertrude's second son. He married Feena "Fanny" Brummel the daughter of Hendrik Brummel and Stijntje Prium in 1889. They had no children. Mart was a farmer and raised dairy cattle and fodder, mostly hay for his cows.. He played an important role in the lives of his sister, Gertrude Dena, and nephews Richard (my uncle) and Jacob (my father.) Mart and Fanny lived in the Zeeland area their whole lives. Mart died at age 69 in 1938; Fanny lived to be 78 and died in 1947. They were buried in Zeeland Cemetery.

3. **Maria "Mary"** (1872-1952): Not long after Dirk's wife Gertrude died, he and his daughter Gertrude Dena traveled to Vernal, Utah, where they lived with Dirk's daughter Mary, her husband Rev. Benjamin Anthony Van Duine, and their children Cornelia and Richard.

Dirk Van Loo and his 11-year-old daughter, Gertrude Dena, after her mother died

**Standing: Dirk and his daughter Gertrude Dena
Seated: Rev. Benjamin Van Duine holding Cornelia, and daughter Mary (Van Loo) Van Duine holding Richard**

Mary had married Benjamin on September 23, 1896. The Van Duines had become missionaries in Utah by 1900. My father, Jack Van Hoven, remembers his mother, Gertrude Dena, telling this story, "When my father and I were in Utah we rode horses, and I rode a horse that was very afraid of Indians. So we crossed this bridge and there on the bank was this group of Indians and the horse turned around and ran home just as quite as he could go. All I could do was hold on.

"Grandpa Van Loo was also shot while in Utah. There was a lot of shooting of course and there was a boy who shot him through the leg with a rifle, by mistake."

After my grandmother, Gertrude Dena, married Henry Van Hoven, both Cornelia and Richard Van Duine lived with Dirk, Gertrude Dena, Henry and family at some time when they were growing up so they could experience Zeeland and the Dutch community.

The Van Duine family lived in many different places. In 1910 they were in Maple Grove, Colorado and Benjamin listed his occupation as farmer. In 1920 he was farming in Payne Delta, Colorado, and by 1930 they had moved to Beaumont, Riverside, California. Benjamin died in Ventura County, California in 1938 at age 63, and Mary died in 1952, in Marysville, Yuba Co., California, at the age of 75.

4. **Cornelis "Corneal"** (1875-1959): In 1900, Dirk and Gertrude Dena were living with Dirk's third oldest son, Corneal, and his wife. Corneal had married Jacomina "Minnie" Korstanje on May 28, 1896. She was the daughter of Anthonie and Wilhelmina Korstanje.

Corneal was a cabinet maker in a furniture factory and later he became the owner and manager of the Zeeland Furniture Factory. Corneal and Minnie had 4 children: Dirk (1897-1937), who was named after his paternal grandfather; Anthony (b. 1899), named after his maternal grandfather, sadly died in 1910 at age 11; Gertrude (1903-1989), who was named after her paternal grandmother, and Wilson (1910-1982).

The caption for this photo reads "Paul Rief and Corneal Vanden Bosch Store. Mr. Rief behind counter, Paul Rief in front. Corneal Vanden Bosch also pictured."

Minnie died on Oct. 19, 1939 at the age of 62 in Holland, and Corneal died on July 13, 1959 in Zeeland at the age 84. They were buried in Pilgrim Home Cemetery in Holland.

5. **Thomas** (1878-1892) was Dirk's fourth and youngest son. He died at age 14.
6. **Gertrude Dena Van Loo** (1888-1952), was 11 at the time of her mother's death, and she was the only child who was living at home at the time. She became the housekeeper for her dad. Later she married **John "Henry" Van Hoven** (1884-1970), and they were my grandparents.

Front row, center: Minnie (Korstanje) and Corneal Van Loo
Back row: Gertrude, Wilson and Dirk

Gertrude Dena as a teenager

In 1914, Cornelius (aged 76) and his brother Dirk (aged 68) returned to Driewegen, the Netherlands, to visit relatives and to see the house in which they had been born.

Dirk Van Loo visits with Mr. De Pree

Cornelius Van Loo, standing in front of the former Van Loo home in Driewegen, the Netherlands

Nellie Van Loo (Mrs. Aart Marteyn and daughter Neeltje Marteyn

Other relatives

CHAPTER 5
Gertrude Dena (Van Loo) Van Hoven's Maternal Ancestry

AS PREVIOUSLY MENTIONED, Gertrude Dena Van Loo (my grandmother) was the daughter of **Dirk Van Loo** (1846-1923) and **Grietje "Gertrude" Vanden Bosch Van Loo** (1848-1899), who were my great-grandparents. Her parents, **Melle Vanden Bosch** (1819-1897) and **Tryntje (Westerbeek) Vanden Bosch** (1820-1902), were my 2nd great-grandparents.

Gertrude Vanden Bosch Van Loo's Maternal Ancestry

- Gertrude's mother, **Tryntje Westerbeek Vanden Bosch,** was the daughter of **Peter Westerbeek** (1786-1874) and **Tallegjen Berends Houwer** (1798-1841), who were my 3rd great-grandparents.
- Peter's parents, **Teunis Pieters Westerbeek** (1750-1817) and **Trijntje Hans Heida** (1751-1840), were my 4th great-grandparents.
- Teunis's parents, **Pieter L. Westerbeek** (1720-?) and **Jibbechien Jannes te Blesdijk** (1730-?), were my 5th great-grandparents.
- Pieter L.'s parents, **Luytien Jans Westerbeek** (1698-?) and **Hendrikjen** ? (1698-?), were my 6th great-grandparents.

Many of the Westerbeeks lived in Drenthe, the Netherlands.

Gertrude Vanden Bosch Van Loo's Paternal Ancestry

Gertrude's father, **Melle Vanden Bosch's**, ancestry can be traced back 10 generations in Friesland, the Netherlands:
- Melle's father, **Tommie Molle Vanden Bosch** (1798-1874), married **Grietje Koenen Bont** (1799-1865); they are my 3rd great-grandparents.
- Tommie's parents, **Melle Tamma Vanden Bosch** (1761-1818) and **Grietje Hanszes** (1767-1842), were my 4th great-grandparents.
- Melle's parents, **Tamme Molles Vanden Bosch** (1726-1824) and **Lutske Jacobs Girbeson** (1730-1807), were my 5th great-grandparents.
- Tamme's parents, **Molles Ottes Vanden Bosch** (1693-1759) and **Antje Johannes** (1699-1743), were my 6th great- grandparents.

- Molles's parents, **Otte Tammes Vanden Bosch** (1665-before1765) and **Janke Molles** (after 1661-before 1761), were my 7th great- grandparents.
- Otte's parents, **Tamme Everts Vanden Bosch** (1635-?) and **Wytske Oenes** (1634-?), were my 8th great-grandparents.
- Tamme's parents, **Evert Hendriks Vanden Bosch** (1604-1672) and **Jouck Tammes** (1605-?), were my 9th great-grandparents.
- Evert's parents, **Hendrik Everts Vanden Bosch** (1575-?) and **Hylck Feddes (1575-?),** were my 10th great-grandparents.

Melle's parents, **Tommie Molle** and **Grietje Koenen Bont Vanden Bosch,** my 3rd great-grandparents, were farmers in the Netherlands. This story about **Tommie Molle** and **Grietje Koenen Bont Vanden Bosch** was told by one of his sons:

"Tommie was married to Grietje Koenen BONT on 7 Mar 1821 in Grieteny, West Stellingwerf (now called Wolvega), Friesland, the Netherlands." (Added by Norma: **Tommie Molle Vanden Bosch** was a 23-year-old farmer living in Peperga, Friesland, and **Grietje Koenen Bont** was a 21-year-old farmer's maid in Peperga.)

Story of Tommie, as told by one of his sons (continued): *"Tommie was with the Seceders in 1821 in Drenthe, Netherlands. Poor and intensely religious, the Vanden Bosch family joined the Secession, a move which probably did not advance their material welfare. He emigrated after March 21, 1821 from Wolvega, Friesland, Netherlands to Havelte, Drenthe, Netherlands. He moved in 1846 from Havelte, Drenthe, Netherlands to Witten, also in Drenthe.*

When the public and the government expressed their ill will toward Seceeders, Tommie talked about emigrating. Just about this time the eldest of his nine children, Koene, was entering upon his ministerial career, but three of Tommie's sons expressed a desire to go to America, whereupon Tommie said to his wife: 'Then we must go with them, for the practice of our faith is free in America, and that is precisely what we desire.' 'Yes,' replied Grietje (Bont), 'but I cannot bring myself to take this step, because Koene cannot go with us, and to leave him here is something I cannot bear.' But father and children, including daughter Grietje, soon decided to emigrate, while mother Vanden Bosch remained reluctant. After she rose one morning, however, she spoke to Tommie: 'Father, now I am ready to go to America . . . . I have prayed to God that He might give me freedom to leave, if it is His will we emigrate to America, and He has indeed given me this freedom, has heard my prayer; I am ready to leave for America!'

In 1848, the Tommie Vanden Bosch family left the little village of Witten, near Assen, in the province of Drenthe. At this time, Tommie was 50 years old and Grietje was 49. Seven of their children came with them but the oldest, Koene, opted to stay behind. First, the family traveled to

Ammersod, located in the province of Gelderland (also in the Netherlands), where they boarded a riverboat to Amsterdam. There they boarded the *Scandia*, debarking at New York on May 29, 1848.

The *Scandia*

With limited means, Tommie and his family made their way to Ottawa County, Michigan, settling in Grand Haven. Later, Tommie and his family were some of the first white settlers to locate near the present city of Zeeland, and there he owned eighty acres of land, on which he spent the remainder of his days.

Grietje Bont Vanden Bosch died on Nov. 24, 1865, at the age of 65. Tommie Vanden Bosch died on Dec. 17, 1874, in Zeeland, Michigan. He was 77 years old. They both were buried on the farm of Mrs. Evers, 2 miles north of Zeeland, Michigan, where they had previously lived.

Historian Marian Schoeland said of the Vanden Bosch family, "They were far from perfect. But they knew the Bible thoroughly, they believed it implicitly; they had found its promises to be true in daily experiences….They loved God and His Word so much that they were ready to suffer persecution and even die rather than consent to the slightest doubt or denial. They were convinced that every aspect of life must be lived to His glory…"

Tommie Vanden Bosch's obituary said of him, "*The community found in this worthy pioneer a faithful and unswerving friend, ever alert to serve its best interest and generous in his contributions toward every movement tending to the general advancement.*"

Tommie Molle Vanden Bosch and Grietje Koenen Bont Vanden Bosch's Children

1. Rev. Koene Vanden Bosch (1818-1897): Since the Vanden Bosch family was very poor, Koene began work as a shepherd when he was 12 to contribute to the family's finances.

    As an adult, Koene had a deep, personal conversion experience with Christ. He said, "Until my 20th year I did not know a God in my heart, nor did I have any self- knowledge. When I was 21, the Lord brought me from death to life, out of darkness into the light." Three years after his conversion he began to study for the ministry.

    Koene was known to be strong-willed and stubborn—some even said he was hot-tempered and stern. He was deeply concerned about the parity of doctrine and life in the church. On the other hand, it was clear that he was also warmly and personally committed to the Lord.

Koene and Jarringjen Vanden Bosch **Rev. Koene Vanden Bosch** **Rev. Vanden Bosch later in life**

In 1834, a minority of the Dutch Reformed Church had seceded, resulting in a split known as the Secession of 1834, or *Afscheiding*. As mentioned previously, the Vanden Bosch family were Seceders, and Koene joined them. He could not approve of the connection of emigrant-communities with the Dutch Reformed Church. This separation meant the start of the Christian Reformed Church in the United States.

Although the Secessionists did not have an educational program for ministers, Koene took lessons from two or three ministers in the province of Drenthe, where he lived. He studied hard to increase his knowledge, taking his books to the moor and reading them while he herded the sheep.

Koene married Jarringjen Rook in 1840 when he was 22, and they had 5 children. Although his parents and siblings emigrated to the United States in 1848, Koene decided to stay in the Netherlands. He became the 3rd minister of a Secessionist church in Noordeloos, the Netherlands, serving in the community of Elburg from 1847-1848. The church did not pay him very much, so Koene and his family were poor. On one Saturday night there was no food in the house, and the young minister asked the Lord what would become of his family because they were so hungry. Before they went to bed, someone knocked on the door and brought a basket full of food!

In 1853 Koene got a call from the Apeldoorn community of Noordeloos and was confirmed in 1854 by Rev. Zeebuyt of Leerdam, and started his ministerial position in Noordeloos with the words of Psalm 51:14-15: *"Deliver me from blood guiltiness, O God, thou God of my salvation, and my tongue shall sing aloud of thy righteousness. O Lord, open thou my lips, and my mouth shall show forth thy praise."* At that time the church had 183 members, who lived in the towns of Noordeloos, Hoogblokland, Hoornaar and Goudriaan.

In 1856, Rev. Koene gave his last sermon in Noordeloos, the Netherlands, for he had accepted a call from the new community Noordeloos in Michigan, the United States, which was named after the Dutch town of the same name. He brought his family and 29 members from his church in the Netherlands to the United States. In West Michigan, as the pastor of the Noordeloos Reformed Church, services were held in the open air; his pulpit was a farmer's wagon and his pulpit chair was a tree stump. That year he was promised a salary of $400, which he wasn't paid fully because the congregants had so little money. He also had to farm to support his family. It was not long before Rev. Koene came to believe that the Reformed Churches in the area were leaving the purity of the church due to their singing of hymns instead of Psalms, their supposed neglect of catechism preaching, and by allowing non-Reformed Christians to take the Lord's Supper. On April 8, 1857, Koene sent a stern letter to the Classis Holland meeting that was held in a Zeeland church. The letter began, "By this…I declare myself no longer to belong to you" and it ended with the strong exhortation, "I hope that your eyes may yet be opened to see your extreme wickedness, to take it to heart, and to be converted therefrom." Nineteen members of the Nordeloos church parted the church, along with Rev. Koene, and about 250 members from Graafschaap, which is in Filmore Township, and Coopersville, which is in Polkton Township. Rev. Koene Vanden Bosch was the only pastor of these churches.

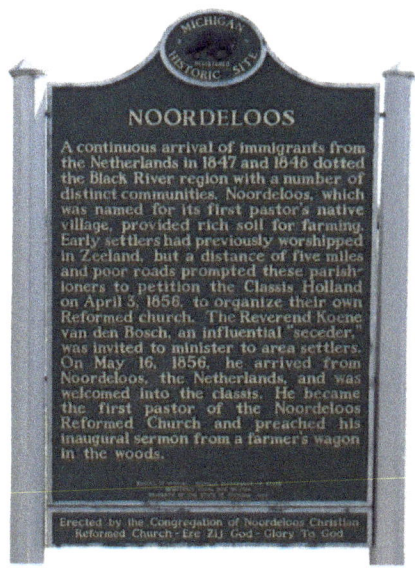

Historical marker, Norderloos Christian Reformed Church, Michigan

Rev. Koene later became a traveling pastor. He was a familiar sight, traveling in a wagon pulled by a team of oxen. He carried with him a shovel and an ax in the wagon box so he could dig the wagon out of ruts, or to clear fallen brush from the road. Often he was seen reading, praying, planning, and singing psalms as he went. Sometimes he was gone for days, ministering to this scattered flock. He wore himself down terribly in those years, lost a great deal financially and was subjected to a great deal of verbal accusations.

And so it was that, under the leadership of Rev. Koene Vanden Bosch in 1857, many people left the Reformed Church in Holland/Zeeland, just as they did in Grand Rapids under the leadership of Rev. Gijsbert Haan. Both men were influential in a new denomination, which was later called the Christian Reformed Church (CRC) of America.

Rev. Koene was also involved in the early days of Calvin College. From 1869-1878 he served at the 1st Christian Reformed Church in Grand Haven, Michigan, and from 1878-1881 he served the 1st CRC church in Chicago, Illinois. He retired in 1881 due to ill health and was granted emeritus status. In 1883 he served on the Christian Reformed Synod.

After Rev. Koene's wife, Jarringjen, died in 1887, he married Tryntje Dekker on October 1, 1888. He died in 1897 at the age of 79, and his second wife, Tryntje, died in 1912 at the age of 89. Koene and Jarringjen were buried in the Lake Forest Cemetery in Grand Haven.

2. **Melle Vanden Bosch** (1819-1897)) and **Tryntje Westerbeek Vanden Bosch** (1820-1902) were my 2nd-great grandparents. See their story in Chapter 6.
3. Pieter Vanden Bosch (1822-1864) married Harmentien Essing on June 23, 1844 in the Netherlands. They had two children. After coming to the United States with his family, Pieter and Harmentein settled in Zeeland on a farm. In 1857, Pieter purchased 18 acres in Ottawa County.

    Harmentien died before 1860 and Pieter married Nielje Stagter. She came to the marriage with five children with the last name of Achterhoof. They had two children. After Nielje died Pieter married Sietske Jans Vande Burg on Dec. 21, 1893. Peiter died on Jan. 18, 1909 at the age of 87.
4. Jacob Vanden Bosch (1824-1910) married Hendrinka Kruims in the Netherlands and they had four children. After coming to the United States, Jacob was a farmer in the Zeeland area. Hendrinka died in 1879 at the age of 56, and Jacob married Amerentia van Strien in 1880. Jacob died on Mar. 8, 1910 at the age of 85 years, and Amerentia died in 1917 at the age of 88.
5. Anneshina "Anne" Hannah Vanden Bosch (1830-1907) married Adrian Benjamin and they lived in Grand Rapids. They had 8 children.

    One of their sons became well known in Grand Rapids. It was written about him, *"Thomas was the son of pioneer Dutch settlers Adrian Benjaminse and Anneshina VandenBosch. A carpenter, he moved to Grand Rapids in 1880 to work in the furniture factories, including Sligh Furniture, and became a foreman at the William Berkey Co. Nine years later, he left the furniture industry to work as a carpenter and builder. His son, architect Adrian Benjamin, joined him in his business in 1904. They built over 150 homes in the Grand Rapids area, as well as commercial buildings, apartment buildings, schools and churches. He laid out and developed both Plymouth and Cambridge Boulevards in East Grand Rapids, and Benjamin Avenue is named after him. A Seventh Day Adventist, he built the Seventh Day Adventist church on Cass Ave. (no longer standing) and designed other churches in Pennsylvania, Florida and Washington, D.C. With Harvey Weemhof as a partner, they also constructed Bethel Christian Reformed Church, among other buildings."*

    Anne died in 1907 at the age of 77, and Adrian died in 1917 at the age of 88. They were buried in Oakhill Cemetery, Grand Rapids.
6. Folleshina Talligje "Tillie" Vanden Bosch (1837-1927) married Jan Scholtin, a farmer near Zeeland, in 1857. Tillie and Jan had 10 children. Jan died in 1913 at the age of 75. and Talligje

died in 1921 at the age of 85 years. They were both buried in Zeeland Cemetery.

7. Grietje Vanden Bosch (1840-1918) married John Henry Boone in 1857. John had come to the Holland area with his parents and the Van Raalte colonists in 1847. He helped to build the Plank Road and became a Pioneer Stage driver on the Kalamazoo – Grand Rapids line. He was soon able to buy a farm near Holland, and he and Grietje lived there for about 23 years, raising 11 children. In about 1894 they moved to Zeeland. John died in 1914 at the age of 77, and his funeral was at the 1st Reformed Church in Zeeland. Grietje died in 1918 at the age of 79. They were both buried in the New Groningen Cemetery.

Jan and Tillie Vanden Bosch Scholtin

Grietje Vanden Bosch Boone

John Henry Boone

8. Johannes Vanden Bosch (1841-1905) was the last child born to Melle and Grietje Vanden Bosch. He married Lyda Kropschot in 1857 in Zeeland, where they farmed and began their family nearby. They had 10 children together.

   In 1877 the family moved to Iowa. There Johannes bought land for $5.00 an acre. He didn't like the prairie land of Iowa, and after a few months the family moved back to Michigan. Lyda died in 1881 at the age of 36 years, leaving 10 children motherless. Her infant son was cared for by a caring friend, but the baby died when he was four months old.

   In 1882 Johannes married Cornelia Vander Heide, and the following year the family moved to Harrison, South Dakota. During the first summer, they lived in a small sod house with a ground floor. Keeping dry during rainy weather was quite a problem. Johannes and Cornelia had 3 children.

The family's next move was to Leota, Minnesota. After a few years they left the Leota community and settled near Pease, Minnesota. The trip from Leota to Pease was made in a covered wagon, which Johannes made himself. From Pease, they moved to Wright County, Iowa, where Johannes died in 1905 at the age of 63. Cornelia died in 1934 at the age of 88. Most of their children settled in Iowa or Minnesota.

**Lyda Kropschot,
Johannes Vanden Bosch's first wife**

**Johannes Vanden Bosch and Cornelia
Vander Heide, his second wife**

The Johannes and Cornelia (Vander Heide) Vanden Bosch Family

**Back row: Peter (1879-1956) and Johanna (1877-1963)
Middle row: Willem (1885-1964); father Johannes (1842-1905) holding Cora; Cornelia, Johannes's second wife (1846-1934) and Johannes (1883-1972)**
Photo courtesy Dave Wyngaarden

CHAPTER 6
The Melle and Tryntje (Westerbeek) Vanden Bosch Story

AS A MARRIED COUPLE, **Melle Vanden Bosch** and **Tryntje Westerbeek Vanden Bosch** set off from the Netherlands, along with his parents and siblings, in 1848. At that time they were, respectively, 29 and 28. They settled in Zeeland, where Melle became a dry goods merchant. He was active and well known in Zeeland, in fact he is also pictured with Cornelius Van Loo in the "Early Pioneers of Zeeland" (photo on page 27).

Melle Vanden Bosch

Sometime after 1880, the family moved to Grand Haven, where again Melle worked as a merchant. See the following 1880 census report for the **Melle and Tryntje Westerbeek Vanden Bosch** family:

1880 Census

Name:	Melle Van Den Bosch
Home in 1880:	Zeeland, Ottawa, Michigan
Age:	60
Estimated Birth Year:	abt 1820
Birthplace:	Holland
Relation to Head of Household	Self (Head)
Spouse's name:	Trijntje
Father's birthplace:	Holland
Mother's birthplace:	Holland
Neighbors:	View others on page
Occupation:	Drygoods Merchant
Marital Status:	Married
Race:	White
Gender:	Male
Household Members:	

Name	Age
Melle Van Den Bosch	60
Trijntje Van Den Bosch	59
Tamme Van Den Bosch	36
Gertrude Van Den Bosch	37
Anna Van Den Bosch	23
Jacob Van Den Bosch	20
Grietje Van Den Bosch	18
Martin Van Den Bosch	17
Appolonia Pijl	17

Melle and Trientje had nine children. Melle retired in 1892 or 1893. Sometime after retiring, Melle and Tryntje moved back to Zeeland. Melle died at the age of 83 and Tryntje died at the age of 81. They were both buried in Zeeland Cemetery.

Melle and Tryintje Vanden Bosch's Children

1. Tamme Vanden Bosch (1843-1913) married Gertrude Van Loo (Cornelius and Dirk Van Loo's sister) Vanden Bosch, on January 1, 1867. That makes Tamme Vanden Bosch my 2nd great-uncle and Gertrude (Van Loo) Vanden Bosch my 2nd great-aunt. Their story is told below.
2. Peter Vanden Bosch (1845-1928) married Gertje "Gertrude" Kok on Mar. 8, 1865, and the family lived in Zeeland until 1882 when they moved to Lucas, Michigan. In 1892 they moved back to Zeeland. Peter and Gertje had 11 children.

While living in Zeeland, Peter served as street commissioner, village marshall (sheriff) and lamplighter. He was also a carpenter, and at one time he worked as a night-watchman at the Zeeland Furniture Factory. When the Interurban line was built, it was Peter's job to ride the train, called a "dummy," and blow the whistle to warn the ground traffic that the Interurban train was coming.

Standing: Jacob, Peter (father), Peter, John
Seated: Trudy (Shoemaker), Richard, Martin, Tom, Gertrude (Wyngarden)

After Gertje died in 1904, Peter married Martha Van Dyk. They lived in New Era, Michigan. Peter died in 1928 at the age of 83 and was buried in the Zeeland Cemetery.

3. **Gertrude (Vanden Bosch) Van Loo** (1848-1925), my great-grandmother, married **Dirk Van Loo**. They were the parents of my grandmother, **Gertrude Dena**, who married my grandfather, **Henry Van Hoven.**

4. Koene Vanden Bosch (1850-1925) married Johanna M. Herweyer in 1874. Koene was a farmer near Zeeland, and they had 5 children. Johanna died on May 26, 1923 at the age of 67, and Koene died on June 6, 1925 at the age of 75.

5. Tallegje "Tillie" Vanden Bosch (1853-1925) married Johannes II "John" Huyser on Jan. 3, 1873. He was a carpenter and also did odd jobs. They lived in Borculo, Michigan. Two of their children lived beyond infancy. Tillie died on Oct. 23, 1925 at the age of 72 years, and John died on Aug. 8, 1943 at the age of 91. They were both buried in Borculo Cemetery.

6. Marie "Mary" Vanden Bosch (1855-1929) married Lucas Huyser on Oct. 20, 1876. They lived in the Zeeland area, where Lucas was a farmer. They had 4 children. Lucas died on June 3, 1922 at the age of 66 and Mary died in 1929 at the age of 74.

7. Anna Vanden Bosch (1857-1884)**:** In 1880, at the age of 23, Anna was still living with her parents. She is said to have married Albert A. VanDyk, but I could find no other records. She may have had one child. Anna died on Mar. 25, 1884 at 26 years old.

8. Jacob Vanden Bosch (1860-1912) married Grietje Mulder on June 4, 1880. He was a farmer in the Zeeland area. The 1919 census shows that he and his family lived in Arkansas, where they were farming. Jacob and Grietje had 8 children. After Jacob died on Jan. 14, 1912 at the age of 52, Grietje and the family moved back to Holland. Grietje became a dressmaker. The 1920 census shows that she lived with her two youngest sons, Melan and Wallace. In 1930 she was living with her third son, John, and his young family. Grietje died on July 1, 1938 at the age of 76.

9. Martin Vanden Bosch (1863-1898) married Johanna O. Van Dyk on Sept 21, 1882. He worked as a store clerk in Zeeland. On Feb. 14, 1898 Martin died at the age of 35 and was buried in Zeeland Cemetery. He left Johanna to raise their four children, ages 4 to 14. Johanna died on Feb. 12, 1903 at the age of 43 when the children were now 9 to 19 years old.

Tamme Vanden Bosch

Tamme Vanden Bosch was industrious. He was a Michigan pioneer. During the Civil War, he served in the Carolina Campaign under General Tecumseh Sherman, Company I, 25th Michigan Infantry and was wounded in battle in 1865.

Tamme fought in the Civil War as a private in the 28th Michigan Infantry, Company I. He was mustered in on Sept. 22, 1862. On Dec. 27 the Regiment engaged in a skirmish with the Confederates. From January 8 to March 26, 1862, they were employed on provost and picket duty and spent much of their time guarding trains. On April 3, 1862 the Regiment arrived in Louisville, Tennessee, and on June 10th Company I, along with companies D, E, F, and K. marched to Green River Bridge, Kentucky. On the morning of July 4, 1862, with less than 350 men, the troops earned an enviable reputation for a gallant defense, repulsing the attack of Confederate general, John Morgan, who led 3,000 men.

After the entire regiment joined together in Lebanon, in May of 1863, they crossed over the mountains to Eastern Tennessee and camped at Louden, Tennessee. Here the Regiment participated in the defense of Kingston, then Mossy Creek, and in the winter they retreated to Knoxville.

Re-equipped, they moved west to join the Georgia Campaign on May 4, 1864. On May 7th the Regiment engaged the Confederates at Tunnel Hill: on May 9, they fought at Rocky Face; on May 14 they fought at Resaca, and then they fought in engagements at the Siege of Atlanta.

Tamme Vanden Bosch

After the fall of Atlanta, the Regiment marched over 1000 miles through Georgia and Tennessee. Upon arriving at Nashville on Dec. 8th they took an active role in the defense of the city; one man in their regiment was killed, and seven were wounded.

They next marched to Dilston, then went by steamer to Cincinnati to board trains for Washington D.C. Then they traveled on steamers to North Carolina to join General Schofield's army in pursuit of General Johnston's fleeing army.

After the surrender of the Confederate Army, the regiment was sent to Salisbury to be mustered out on the 24th of June 1865, then sent by rail to Michigan. They arrived in Jackson on the 2nd of July, where they were paid off and disbanded.

After serving in the Civil War, Tamme worked as a tinsmith and a teacher. He married Grietje (Gertrude) Van Loo, Cornelius's sister, in 1867; they adopted two children: a boy, Jake Hofman, and a girl, Gertrude, who later married John Mokma.

Tamme later attended Calvin Theological Seminary and was ordained in 1879. For 3 years, he served as a "traveling preacher," working short term in congregations from Ohio to Montana. In 1889 Tamme was appointed the CRC's first missionary, and he and Gertrude worked on the Redbud Indian Reservation in South Dakota for 2 years. The Wounded Knee Massacre was fought in 1890 while they were there, when the Indians (Native Americans) of the Ghost Dance religion came to the Pine Ridge Reservation. When soldiers came and attacked them, they tried to escape through the Badlands, but over 300 men, women and children were killed.

In 1890 Tamme and Gertrude returned to Michigan, and Tamme served in a church in Vriesland. After serving in several more churches, he retired from a church in Three Oaks, Michigan in 1910, at which time he was also an agent for the Chicago Tract Society.

Later in Tamme's life, a petition was distributed in southern Michigan, seeking his commitment to the insane asylum that specialized in depression and sleep difficulties.

At the age of 69, Rev. Vanden Bosch died in 1913 in Kalamazoo, Michigan. Gertrude went to live with her daughter in Holland, where she died in 1918 of stomach cancer at the age of 76. Both Rev. Tamme and Gertrude were buried in Zeeland Cemetery.

The storefront of Gerrit's Dry Goods Store, on the corner of 3rd Street and Columbus, Grand Haven, Michigan, 1885

CHAPTER 7
The Story of Henry and Gertrude Dena (Van Loo) Van Hoven

Henry and Gertrude Dena (Van Loo) Van Hoven's wedding photo

HENRY VAN HOVEN and **Gertrude Dena (Van Loo) Van Hoven**, my grandparents, were married on March 7, 1907, in Zeeland, Michigan. They had five children:

- my father, **Jacob "Jack"** (1908-1998)
- Richard (1909- 1988)
- Irene (1911-1999)
- Gertrude (1913-1990)
- 12 years later a tag-along, Donald (1925-1988), was born.

My grandparents' first children: my father, Jacob, and Richard

Standing: Richard and Jacob
Seated: Gertrude and Irene

Four generations: My grandfather Henry is holding his firstborn, my father, Jack. Also pictured are Irene (Wentzel) Van Hoven and Johannes Wentzel.

Zeeland, 1919
Image courtesy Wikimaedia Commons

A Van Hoven Family Reunion was held soon after Henry and Gertrude were married. Back row: Henry is 4th from the left and Gertrude is beside him. Middle row: Abram and Kate Van Hoven are 1st and 2nd from the left. Front row: adults 5 & 6 are Irene Wentzel Van Hoven and Jacob Van Hoven; adults 7 & 8 are Irene's parents, Agatha and Johannes Wentzel, and adults 9 and 10 are Jacob's parents, Magdalena (Haan) Van Hoven and Abram J. Van Hoven.

Early in their marriage, Henry and Gertrude Dena lived in three different homes in Zeeland. First, they lived with Henry's parents, **Jacob and Irene Van Hoven,** at 27 South Centennial Street. My father, Jack, remembered their move to the second house when he was three years old. As he told it, "I was sitting in the wagon and my father, Henry, was walking on the spokes of the wheels of the wagon as we went along. That was quite an athletic feat." Jack also recalls that the family moved to the third house just before he started kindergarten. Both the second and third houses belonged to Dirk Van Loo, Gertrude Dena's father.

That third house had three bedrooms: Dirk slept in the downstairs bedroom, Henry and Gertrude had an upstairs room, Jack and his brother Dick had the third bedroom, and the two girls, Irene and Gertrude, slept in the large hallway landing at the top of the stairs. The big room by the downstairs entrance was the living room/dining room and it had a coal stove. The large kitchen also had a stove. The parlor, a smaller room at the front of the house, was used mostly when visitors came. The family's one small bathroom was located in what had been a downstairs closet off the kitchen. I remember Grandpa Henry's wonderful garden at the third home, even though he only had a small amount of land. He grew vegetables that climbed up poles and even had room for flowers.

My grandparents' third house

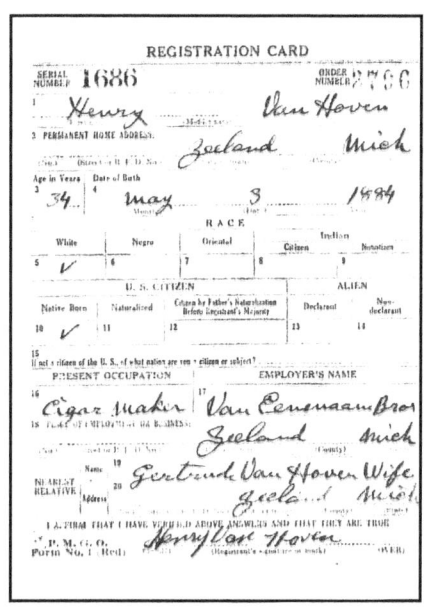

This registration card from the year 1918 shows Henry Van Hoven's occupation as cigar maker.

One day, after Dad began going to school, the Van Hoven family went to the Holland Fair in a hired surrey, which was a buggy with two seats. The family didn't have horses of their own; only wealthy people had their own little barn with a horse. There was a sizable livery stable in town, so if people traveled any distance they hired a horse and buggy.

Most of the time, people walked to where they needed to go. My great-grandfather, **Jacob Van**

Hoven, had horses because of his business. He sold farm machinery, walking plows, drags, etc. There were no tractors then. Also he had a hardware store. They sold stoves in the hardware store after his son Leonard came home from Lansing and worked in the store. Jack also worked there when he was in high school.

My grandfather, Henry Van Hoven, worked at a cigar factory until cigars were rolled by machines.

15 million chicks were raised annually in the hatchery. Both my grandfather Henry and my father Jack worked here on a seasonal basis.

Dad's family went to North St. Christian Reformed Church. At that time, everyone went to church; it was just expected. Cars displayed a white piece of fabric in the windows to show they were just using their car to go to and from church. Since Sundays were considered the days of rest, the family mostly stayed home and did not drive the car other than for going to church. There was extra time for reading, and when the kids got older they would play cards, or checkers and caroms. There was always time for music; Mother Gertrude Dena would play the organ, and everyone would sing. Sometimes neighbors would join them for a sing-along.

When the Van Hoven family emigrated, they took with them a huge Dutch Bible that was printed in 1719. The first Van Hoven birth was recorded in 1730. Many Dutch people did not have last names back then, but the Van Hovens did. Van Hoven means "of gardens." **Abram Van Hoven,** my 2nd great-grandfather, passed the Bible to his oldest son, **Jacob**. It was said that the Wentzel family had somehow gotten hold of the Van Hoven family Bible, and Jacob went to their house and stole it back. Jacob would have passed it down to his oldest son, but since Abram did not have any children it was passed down to his second son, John "Henry". From there it came down to my father, Jacob "Jack" Van Hoven, and now my bother, Richard Van Hoven has it. His son, Jack, and grandson, Seth, are next in line.

Dad was eight years old when World War I began, and he mostly remembers soldiers coming and going. Men from Zeeland often served in Russia. When they returned home, they marched down the streets in Holland. Girlfriends and others ran into the street to greet them.

Standing: Seth Van Hoven; Seated: Jack Van Hoven and Richard Van Hoven, 1996

World War I servicemen are celebrated in a parade in Holland, Michigan

Gertrude Dena's father, **Dirk Van Loo**, lived with Gertrude Dena and Henry for most of their married lives, and their children got to know him well. When Dirk died, he left them the house. When I asked my father, Jack, what held the home together, he said that Grandpa Dirk Van Loo had a lot to do with it. He also said, "Grandpa Van Loo was the finest Christian I ever knew; he was very Christ-like."

Dirk loved children and was very good with them. Much of the home revolved around him. He would be up without fail at 4:00 a.m. and would have the stove going so the house was warm when everyone else got up. By the time mother Gertrude Dena got up, the potatoes were all peeled for the day. All the children looked up to their Grandpa Dirk for quite a lot of things. Jack said, "He had no ambitions to be well-to-do. He just worked for and cared for the family."

Jack wrote this about his grandfather: *"My Grandfather Van Loo had a greater influence on my life than any other person I have ever known. From him I learned tolerance, but most importantly I learned to respect all other people.*

"Grandpa Van Loo always appeared to be old to me. His hair was pure white and receded off his forehead; he kept it trimmed to a medium length. He had a full mustache and a long, wiry, bushy white beard that covered his chin and cheeks and cascaded onto his chest. But his most noticeable features were his pale blue eyes that came to life when he spoke. And unlike so many adults, he nearly always spoke with you, not at you. He was not as big a man as most of the men in our family, and he walked with a slight stoop. But neither his age, nor his size, nor his infirmities slowed him down much. He was lively and because he was retired, he had time for us children. He took the time and interest to help us build camps, take us fishing, and teach us boys how to shoot. Although he was a small man, his hands were broad and sturdy. They seemed to be made for woodworking, which he loved. His mind was quick and creative; he once fashioned a pair of downhill skis for me out of hardwood by shaping the wood and wetting it to bow the skis properly.

Having those skis was a real thrill for me, because everyone else had only homemade barrel skis.

"Grandpa Van Loo was soft-spoken, and treated everyone with kindness and consideration. When he did have something to say, people listened because everyone seemed to know that Grandpa Van Loo was fair, reasonable, and almost always right as well."

Dirk worked part-time as a carpenter and gardener. When shingles would fall off the steep church roof, Grandpa Van Loo would climb up and replace them. When this happened, Jack remembered that his mother would be very concerned because she knew that Dirk was getting older and that he had no business on the roof. He was always helping others out.

Dad told us that, even though Dirk did work part time on and off, he always had time for him and Richard. Dirk thought it was good for boys to be familiar with woodworking, so the boys were almost always building something. If they had trouble and didn't know how to do something, Grandpa Van Loo was always there to help.

My father said, "He let us boys use his tools, and although we were not very careful with them and lost some things, he never complained. Maybe he should have been a little more strict; if he had been, we probably would have learned to take care of our own tools." Dirk kept his ice skates in the workshop. The blades could be attached to his wooden shoes. Jack claimed them when Dirk passed away, and now I have them. They have seen better days, but they are treasured.

Dirk's Van Loo's ice skates

Dad remembered, "The only time I ever saw Grandpa Van Loo angry in my life was when I sassed my mother. I was a good-sized boy at that time. Grandfather was so angry that he was shaking. He shouted "Come here!" to me, but I was rebellious so I ran the other way. He took off after me and we ended up running circles around the house. Of course he couldn't catch me!

But then suddenly I realized that Grandpa Van Loo wasn't behind me anymore. My curiosity soon got the best of me, and I quietly peeked into the dining room. Grandpa Van Loo was sitting quietly on a straight-backed chair, and I could see tears streaming down his checks. My defiance was instantly deflated. There he sat, a small man, not much larger than me. Something stronger than a magnetic pull drew me toward him. By the time I reached his side, I was crying too. As big as I was, I crawled into his lap and buried my face in his scratchy beard. I could feel his shoulders quivering, and he held me in his arms. All he said was, 'Oh, Jakey, oh, Jakey." I had learned my lesson. I was determined never to sass my mother again. And I think Grandpa Van Loo sensed that I had learned my lesson, so he forgave me..

Grandpa Van Loo was very gentle, and he left a wonderful impression on me. He was rather easy going, but he certainly gave all of us a lot of love and attention."

Dirk was loved by many family members and friends in Zeeland. Two of his grandsons, Dick

Van Dyne and Rich Van Hoven, were named after him,. One of the highlights of his life was in 1914, when he (at age 68) and his brother Cornelius (at the age of 76) went back to Driewegen, the Netherlands, to visit relatives and see the house where they were born. He died in 1923 at the age of 76, when Jack was a sophomore in high school.

Grandfather Dirk Van Loo (right) and grandsons Dick Van Dyne and Rich Van Hoven, who were named after him.

Martin and Fanny (Brummell) Van Loo

On May 8, 1889, Uncle Mart (Marinus) Van Loo married Fanny Brummel, daughter of Hendirkus Brummel and Marianus Van Lot, in Leland, Michigan. They had a good-sized farm, and since they did not have any children, their nieces and nephews became important in their lives. Several Van Loo cousins lived there to help with the farming from time to time. Jack lived there every summer from the time he was 8 years old until he graduated from high school to work on the farm. His first job of the day was to milk two of the cows, while Uncle Mart milked the remaining six. At 9:00 a.m., he brought coffee to the field for the workers. Then at noon he brought them lunch, and at 3:00 p.m. he brought more coffee and a snack. Soon Jack also began to feed the cows and the pigs. Uncle Mart did his field work with the horses.

Jack said, "When I was younger, I would drive the horses for the loading of hay. I had to go real slow, but Uncle Mart's horses always wanted to go fast. When pulling the reins to make them slow down, I felt like my arms were going to be pulled off.

"In those days, I had my own pair of wooden shoes. After we did our chores, we'd put our wooden shoes by the back door and come in for breakfast. Then, after breakfast, we'd put on our regular shoes to work in the fields."

Uncle Mart was always singing. He led the singing at church when the organ broke down. He was always good to Gertrude Dena and Henry's family; at the end of work one summer, he gave Jack a suit, and at the end of another summer he gave Jack a bike.

At the table, Fanny always read the Scripture in Dutch, and then Uncle Mart would pray. Jack said, "My Uncle Mart was a fine man, and he was widely respected. We thought he was well-to-do, but when he died we found out that he really didn't have that much. One of the reasons was because he was always helping others, including our family. Yes, Uncle Mart was a nice man. Aunt Fanny was very different, and was always critical. I don't think Uncle Mart could do anything right for her. She was almost entirely deaf, and as I grew up I realized that being hard of hearing made her a tough row to hoe. She was good enough to us boys."

Richard, Henry and Gertrude Dena's second son and Irene, their third child, both contracted polio. Richard was about 2½ years old and Irene was only one. Irene got over it with no lasting effects, but Richard had it worse. He could not use either of his feet well, and his ankles were twisted sideways. Only one of his legs was functioning, and he used to "walk" around the house using his hands. When Richard started school he rode a tricycle, pumping with his one good foot. In the winter, Jack would pull him to school on a sled.

Jack said, "How I used to hate it when people shoveled their sidewalks, especially when Richard was as big as me. I'd have to get a good running start where it was slippery and then pull really hard over the bare sidewalk."

Later, when Richard was in high school, he needed to have some surgeries, but his parents could not afford it. So Gertrude Dena's brother, Uncle Mart, graciously paid; Richard's feet and ankles were straightened, and his tendons were repaired. After the surgery he could walk, although he limped.

It was common at this time that children contracted chicken pox, mumps and measles. When illness struck, families needed to quarantine; the children had to stay home from school, but the parents were still able to work. As it happens in families with multiple children, the child who initially became ill passed the infection on to the other siblings, one after the other. As a result, the children missed a lot of school. The rules were strict during quarantine: a red sign (about 15" long and 6" wide) was displayed outside the quarantined family's house. However, if two families in a neighborhood had children with chicken pox, the children were allowed to play together.

Jack said, "Mother ran the home, and she was the disciplinarian. If we were naughty enough, she would put us in a clothes closet and shut the door. So there we sat in the dark, eventually bawling a lot. When we begged to be let out, Mother would only do so if we promised that we would behave better in the future. On the other hand, our dad didn't do much disciplining but when he did, it was a little bit rough. When he spoke, we obeyed immediately, which we didn't always do with our mother. But the whole home was covered by my grandfather. Grandpa Van Loo let Henry and Gertrude Dena discipline the children, but when he spoke up everybody listened to his wisdom.

Jack remembers two funeral coaches coming to the neighborhood, along with a hearse coach. The first coach was loaded with people and started down the road. The second coach was also loaded with people, but the horses wouldn't start so the men got out, took off their coats, and went to work. They tried several things, like putting sand on the horses' feet to get them going. Well, they did get going but they really took off around the corner and "rammed into the first coach like crazy." Jack and the other neighbors just stood there "with their mouths open" as they watched.

Jack's Grandfather Dirk had guns, and he taught Jack to use his shotgun and rifle. Jack said, "I now own his double-barrel shot gun, because he left it to me when he died. One day we were down in the gravel pits, which was a big thing. That's where we built some of our shacks. We were shooting at tin cans, and Grandpa was trembling in his old age. When he held the gun, the gun barrel would circle around at the end because he was so unsteady; he had trouble aiming, but he always hit the can. That day we were shooting at the cans and the rifle was laying on the bank. My younger brother Rich got ahold of it, and suddenly the shotgun went off. Good thing it wasn't pointed toward us. That time we got a lecture.

"I remember one time we built a shack out of old lumber across the road in Kooly Smits' backyard. We spent a lot of our time there. My dad was a cigar maker, so there were always a lot of cigars around the house. One day we had a bunch of them, and we boys were all smoking cigars. I couldn't have been more than ten at the time. Because we didn't want our mothers to smell the smoke on our breath, we had the bright idea that we would eat some sugar to mask the smell. We already felt sick after smoking, but when we put that sugar on top of that smoke, we were really sick. And soon our mothers knew all about it.

"With the neighborhood boys, we also built a boat out of house siding. The bottom was made from flooring boards. We used tar-covered rags to plug the holes. When we finished, we decided to take the boat to the water to try it out, even though it was raining. So we put on raincoats and boots, and went to the pond.

"A couple of us boys took the boat out, and we paddled like mad in the narrowest area. When we finally got to the other side of the pond, we got out and tipped the boat over to get all the water out. We took turns riding back and forth. Once, the wind became strong, and the waves were four inches high. My dad was with us that day, and he was the last person to ride across. The boat drifted from the narrow crossing and took in too much water. Dad could see he wasn't going to make it to the other side, but that was no problem; he jumped out, and the water only came up to his waist. He waded to the other side with his boots full of water. In the summer, the lake was drained and we saw that there was a deep hole right in the middle of the crossing. Dad had bailed out right at the edge of the hole. Afterwards he said that he would've never made it if he had bailed out over the hole because he couldn't swim."

"In the winters we went ice skating on the pond, along with the whole community. We skated a lot in the daytime, but in the evening the older folks would join us. When the adults built a great big bonfire on the shore, we had some light that allowed us to skate throughout the evening.

"We lived just a skip and a jump from the hill, so when the conditions for sledding were good, the hill was filled with little boys and girls with their sleds. The older kids had a bobsled that could carry five, six, or seven kids.

"One winter, we built a lean-to in the woods. First, we asked the landowner for permission, and he said it would be okay. We stripped an evergreen tree of all its branches and made our shack out of that. The owner helped us pull a little sheet metal stove over to the shack, using our sleds. We had a good time in that shack, and the owner joined us. One day, our stove got too hot; the evergreen was quite dry, so our shack caught fire and burned up.

"In the summer, when our work was done, the neighborhood kids would gather on the corner and play Run Sheep Run. We divided into two teams—one team hid and the other team tried to find them. The members of the team that was hiding would call out signals to the other members to let them know how close they were to being found. The spot that was designated as safe was under the light on the corner, and we would try to run to safety without getting caught.

"We also played baseball and Bull in the Ring. In Bull and the Ring, everyone would hold hands, standing in a circle, with one person in the center. That person would try to break through the ring.

"Playing marbles was really popular also. We would place a large marble on a line, and the goal was to hit it. We'd stand on another line and roll our marble at the big marble, and if we hit it, the big marble was ours.

"Another game we played was Dock on a Rock. A small rock was placed on a big rock, we would stand behind a line and throw another small rock at the "dock." If we hit it, it was ours. This could be a bit dangerous, though. Once someone else's rock hit Dad on the head when he was picking up his dock."

The Henry and Gertrude Dena Van Hoven family was close-knit, and when the kids grew up they developed different interests. Some of these interests were passed on from their parents and other relatives.

Jack remembered two important things about their home life. The first one was that their mother, Gertrude Dena, read to the kids.

Jack said, "I don't imagine that there were very many nights that my mother didn't sit down after supper and read to the four of us. She was very expressive, and she could make a story come alive."

The second thing was the singing. He remembered, "Mother played the organ and we sang as a family. Then, often on Sunday afternoons, neighbors would come and everyone sang together. That was a real fine time for me."

Music was always important to the family. Both Jack and Irene had violins. Jack remembers paying $5.60 for his violin. Irene's violin was higher quality, so it was probably more expensive.

Gertrude had a guitar, and the girls sang and played in a hillbilly band when they got older.

Jack was very active in high school, and he played on lots of sports teams. As a senior, he played baseball, football and basketball. In the fall of 1925, his teammates found out that Jack's mother was expecting. They bought rattles, little toys, and even diapers for the baby. They intended to embarrass Jack, but there wasn't much that could bother him. Donald was born on November 28, 1925.

Gertrude and Irene

Jack's closest friend in high school was Gerrit, but after high school he lost track of him. They played on all the ball teams together and would go fishing together. They had just enough guys to make a team at their school. His graduating class had 36. Basketball was his worst game. He played center. He was always remembered for basketball though because he was so tall. He played all the positions in baseball. In football he remembers one game where he caught the ball to win the game.

Jack's football team; He is in the third row, second from right.

Fourth Row (left to right)—O. Yntema, N. Lanning, G. Veneklasen, E. Van Enam, S. De Pree, A. Lewis.
Third Row (left to right)—C. Van Koevering, W. De Jonge, E. Lanning, M. Ver Plank, J. Van Hoven, L. Volkers.
Second Row (left to right)—R. Plewis, J. Van Dam, Mr. L. J. De Pree (coach), C. Hecox (captain), J. Bouma, J. Wyngarden, D. Keppel.
Front Row (left to right)—G. Schermer, J. Van Dorple, L. De Vries, R. Madderom.

The students' relationships with the teachers were excellent. My father admitted that he did not study much. He said, "I don't think I would have ever passed Latin if my cousin wasn't the teacher." He recalled an English teacher who took him aside and gave him a project in order for him to pass the class; Jack did the project and got a C. Sometimes he and his friends gave their teachers a hard time. Once, while on a hike during one of their classes, the teacher said they had to be back in school at a certain time. Dad and Gerrit waited until the last second to come in.

Sometimes the kids would put the chalkboard eraser on the teacher's (or someone else's) seat so they would get chalk on their pants when they sat down.

Jack said, "All through high school I worked in the hatcheries, all day on Saturdays, and usually on Friday when there wasn't a ballgame. On Sundays I would go in at midnight and work until 7:00 a.m., and then I would go to school. I was permitted to miss school during these work times. Once, I was scheduled to speak at the pep rally in the morning for one of the events that was schedule that night. I had been at work and I came late, so I peeked into the assembly room door through the glass. One of the cheerleaders saw me and she ran out to get me, but I ran into the boy's room and stayed there.

"I took singing and speech. All the students had to give a prepared speech, and although I had prepared mine, I didn't expect to give it since my last name was Van Hoven, and only one student, Joanne Vand, came after me alphabetically. But instead of starting at the beginning of the alphabet, the teacher started at the end. She called on Joanne, but Joanne wasn't prepared. Then she called on me. Joann had given me an idea, and I thought that was a nice out so I just said "Unprepared." After that day, when the teacher called on Joanne and me, we would say "Unprepared." Other students would also claim to be unprepared of course, and after a couple of days the teacher said, "I'm going to take 5% off your mark if you are not prepared." I waited until after everyone else had given their speech, and then I finally had to give mine.

A lot of memories from school were a little on the funny side. In our history class, there were three rows of chairs with desks on the side. The teacher had me sitting in the front row and Ray Brummel sat right behind me. Another boy sat in the back row, and we all kind of leaned back in our chairs. I lost my balance and went over backwards, and then all three of us landed on the floor."

Jack's baseball team: he is standing at the far right.

From the 1927 Zeeland High School Year Book:

Jack Van Hoven's chosen quote:
"Deeds are better things than words are"

Born in Zeeland
Attended Zeeland Public Schools
Football – 2,4
Baseball – 2,3,4
Letter Club – 2,3,4
Basketball – 3,4
Radio Club – 2,3
Tennis – 3
Glee Club – 4

Voted the Senior Most Athletic Boy

My father's high school graduation photo

Jack and his friends, or sometimes his sisters, liked to go to Grand Rapids on the interurban train that began running in 1901. The interurban first began running in 1898 from downtown Holland to Lake Macatawa.

Jack recalled, "The Interurban regularly ran several times a day. It was a single car, of course, and it ran on electricity. There was an overhead pole with a wheel that was attached on a wire, and the current came from there. A train station was in the Zeeland/Holland business district. The Interurban was used much more than the

The Interurban Train

regular, larger train because it was a local thing. It started in Grand Rapids, went through Grandville, Jamestown, Vriesland, then Zeeland to Holland. It ended in what was then called Jenison Park, which was an amusement center at the lakeshore. We had our Sunday School picnics at Jenison Park, so the Interurban was really the only way we could get there. I can remember that we liked to go out there and put pennies on the Interurban track to have them squashed.

Dad said, "My uncle Mart had one of the earliest automobiles, a 1913 Ford. The tires did not hold air very well, and on Saturdays my job was always to pump those tires up. And I hated that to beat the band. I have no recollection of learning to drive, but I can remember very well trying to teach my dad to drive. He was driving along pretty well, and then he got mixed up about what he had to do just as we were north of Borculo. The ditches were about ten feet deep; he wasn't paying attention, and he started to cross the road right toward that great big ditch. Between our seats there was a hand brake, and I pulled that hand brake hard to stop us.

"My first car was a 1923 Ford Roadster. My dad and I were running incubators in Lansing, and while I drove us there on a snowy day, one of the side windows broke out. That was a long and cold trip. I wrecked it one night when I banged up my car and my neighbor's as well.

"At Christmas we would cut our own tree and string cranberries and popcorn on it. Sometimes we made popcorn balls for decorations also. Our family 'never had any money' so my mother, your Grandma Van Hoven, would borrow from the bank to buy Christmas presents and then pay it back later with household funds. With some of the borrowed money, she bought overcoats with fur collars for Rich and me. One Christmas my dad got his first watch. I don't think Grandma ever told Grandpa about borrowing money. Lots of visiting was done over Christmas and New Years. Also, there was considerable drinking. Budiyungus, made with rum and raisins, was a favorite. Hollanders had no opposition to drinking."

In 1927 Jack graduated from Zeeland High School. He was already working in the hatchery at times, but it wasn't long before he got a job in Grant, Michigan as a bookkeeper. Then he got a job working in the Heines Receiving Station in Ensley, Michigan. While living there, he met Mildred Allyne Cook (1911-1998), who lived in Ensley Center with her parents, George Cook (1886-1969) and Bertha Green Cook (1886-1965). Mildred graduated from 8th grade from the Ensley Center School. She had done well in school and would have liked to continue to high school, but there was not a high school in Ensley Center. She would have needed a ride to the high school in Grand Rapids. There were a few boys in Ensley Center who drove to the Grand Rapids high school, but her father did not want her riding to school with boys. Instead, she found work as a child caregiver. As she got older, she worked in Grand Rapids as a caregiver and then for the telephone company.

The Henry VanHoven Family, circa 1934

Standing: Irene "Ikie," Jacob "Jack", Donald, Richard "Dick", Gertrude "Gertie"
Seated: mother Gertrude Dena, father John "Henry"

CHAPTER 8
The Story of Jack and Mildred (Cook) Van Hoven

MY FATHER TOLD this story about how he met my mother: "I was working in the Heines Receiving Station, which was on the corner. A man called Car worked with me, and he arranged for me to go on a date with Mildred to a young people's meeting at Ensley Center Baptist Church. Car had plans to meet up with Mildred's friend, Gerodean Larson.

As Mildred recalled it, "I lived at home that summer. I always had the car for young people's meetings, and I would pick up Gerodean on the way. But that night my mom needed to have the car. Gerodeen said that she would get us to the meeting, and that Jack would walk me home."

Jack said, "It was a long walk, too. It was 2½ miles from the church to Mildred's home, and then I had to walk 3½ miles back to where I was boarding. My first impression of Mildred was very positive, and I was smitten. Oh ya, there wasn't any doubt in my mind, as soon as I got to know her. Some people propose one time, but I just proposed all the time until Mildred finally said 'yes.' "

When Mom was asked about that first date she said, "I knew he was in the area, but I don't think I had ever seen him until that first date. I wasn't very enthusiastic. When I got home I had to get some things and then go to Grand Rapids, and I was kind of late."

My parents while dating

At some point during the time that my parents were dating, Jack lived and worked in Zeeland, which meant a longer drive home. He tells of one scary time: "One night, when I was going down Grandville Avenue with my Ford coupe (the one with a rumble seat), I had an accident. It happened so quickly. I remember seeing the car ahead of me and the car behind me, but I don't remember in between. I fell asleep and my coupe went flying across the street. I went up a curb right by the guard rail, and the car ran into a lamp post and knocked it over. That about ruined the front of my car. I went to the fire station and called my Uncle Abe, who came and got me.

"After that, to stay awake I would stand on the running board, hook one arm over the top of the door, and steer the car with my other hand. I would go 50 miles per hour or more, because you could go fast on those roads.

Mildred had a positive impact on Jack's faith. He said, "The Reformed Church was an evangelist church, but evangelism was not the emphasis in the Christian Reformed Church. Members of the CRC believed strongly in the doctrine of divine election. If you were born into a CRC family you were a covenant child, so missionary endeavors and evangelist activity was almost nil. The only time we really heard the Gospel in a Christian Reformed Church was when nonmembers came to the church, for example for a funeral or another event. It was thought that CRC church members didn't need to hear the Gospel, you see. In the Reformed Church, evangelistic meetings were held every year, and they were good meetings."

My mother,
Mildred Allyne Cook

When I was a boy there were already schools that were supported by CRC churches. We, of course, belonged to the Christian Reformed Church, and there was considerable pressure for families to send their children to these schools but we went to the public school. I remember a family down the street from us; their son graduated from the eighth grade in the Christian school. The only Christian high school was in Holland, and the parents couldn't possibly afford to send him there. At first the parents were going to send him to the public school, but because of the pressure from the church they changed their minds, so he didn't go to high school at all."

"The official songs of the CRC were solely psalms, mostly sung in English. No hymns were sung in church, so at home we sang mostly psalms also. When we were kids, we went to Catechism, where we spoke both Holland and English. Many kids didn't know enough English to have their questions and answers in English. However, no Dutch was spoken in our home so we were fluent. Grandfather Van Loo insisted that we speak English because we lived in America. We didn't learn much Dutch language, but my brother Rich and the girls could read Dutch.

"At the time I met Mildred, I was not yet saved; meeting Mildred and my salvation all took place in the same year. But not long after that, I was very much under conviction while working in Ensley. One of my first dates with Mildred was going to a prayer meeting. Many things that led up to my salvation happened at the Ensley Church. It kind of scared me when an evangelist talked about the end days. He said that the end of the world was supposed to come, according to his figures, in 1932. Well in 1932 I knew that I was lost, and I didn't know how to be saved. It wasn't long after that, while I was under conviction, that Mildred was able to quote to me from memory Romans 10: 9 and 10: *That if thou shalt confess with thy mouth the Lord Jesus, and shalt believe in thine heart that God hath raised Him from the dead, thou shalt be saved. For with the heart man believeth unto righteousness; and with the mouth confession is made unto salvation.* Because of my church background, along with hearing that verse, my eyes were opened.

"Afterward, when Mildred and I were still going together, I attended the evangelistic services at Zeeland Reformed Church, and I accepted the Lord as Savior. I also made my Confession of Faith in the Reformed Church."

My parents met in September of 1932 and my mother accepted Dad's proposals in April of 1933. They were married on August 25, 1933, with Rev. John Douglas of Ensley Center Baptist Church officiating.

My parents' engagement was quite an event in the community, and Mildred had several showers before the wedding. Jack and Mildred were married at her Grandmother Green's house. Mildred wore a gown of beautiful peach crepe and carried a bouquet of white roses. Jack's sister Gertrude, as the maid of honor wore a green crepe dress and carried a bouquet of white asters and red roses. Mildred's brother Leo stood up with them as best man. Following the service, a bounteous wedding supper was served to the assembled guests.

When Jack and Mildred were ready to leave, a group of young men tried to detain them. Night had not yet fallen, and the young men wanted to do a *shivaree* after Jack and Mildred were in bed. Shiverees were common in those days; wedding guests would often visit the newlyweds' home on the night of the wedding and play practical jokes on them.

First, while Jack and Mildred were still at Grandma Green's house, the guests let all the air out of the tires of Jack and Mildred's car. Jack refilled the tires and the newlyweds got ready to go, but they found that they could not get out of Grandma Green's driveway. The driveway was a "cut road," and it was so narrow that only one car could go down it at a time. There were steep sides all the way down. It turned out that one of the young men had driven his car into the cut road and was blocking it. Jack's brother Dick banged his car into the car that was blocking the driveway, but that didn't work. They finally called the State Police from a neighbor's house across the street, and the policemen came and made the young man move his car.

Left: my parents; Right: my mother

Finally, Jack and Mildred drove to their first home in Drenthe. Their friends did do a shiveree that night, but it was friendly. Jack and Mildred left out candy and cigars and the people who came made some noise and took the candy and cigars, but they did not do any damage.

Jack and Mildred's first home was on the Bos Poultry Farm, about two miles southeast of Zeeland, near Drenthe. Mr. Bos had moved a lot of chickens to the property, and Jack was in charge of taking care of them. The newlyweds' house was square, with four equal-sized rooms. There was a living room, a bedroom and a kitchen, and another room where junk was stored.

Jack and Mildred shopped for furniture together. The total cost was $225, and they paid $12 a month until it was paid off. For part of the year, Jack was making only $1 a day in the celery fields. Jack said, "Our furniture included a davenport, a chair, a couple end tables, a kitchen table and chairs, and the bed and dresser. That was it, except for Mildred's hope chest. We had a rug in the living room and linoleum in the kitchen."

Jack worked a lot on their kitchen. He said, "I built a sink, and the pump went right down through the floor into the basement. The well was also in the basement. I was quite proud of that sink. We had a gasoline stove in the kitchen, which was fancy for those days. After Jack painted three rooms of the house, it was finally time to move in. The corner of that house had been smashed in, but Jack patched it together as well as he could.

Cellars in those days were not like basements of today. There were all kinds of newspapers and other trash in Jack and Mildred's basement, so they avoided it. Jack said, "There was always an awful lot of racket down there. We found out later that black snakes were chasing mice in the basement. I killed the snakes in the yard some time later." The newlyweds were grateful that they had a good door between the basement and the upstairs.

Jack and Mildred lived in that house less than a year. When asked about their first year of marriage, Jack said, "No real problems. I can remember that. We lived in a time when people were really poor. The Depression started in 1928 with a bang, of course. President Roosevelt was elected in 1932, when Mildred and I were dating. I remember listening to the politicians' speeches when I was working in Big Rapids for the Kraft Heinz Company. Many people were out of work, so it was really a tough time. There was a time when you were allowed 16 hours of work for 40 cents an hour, which was the standard rate. It wasn't always possible to get jobs like that, and I worked for $1 a day all fall and winter. I made $27.46 a week at Heinz, and $30 a week in the hatchery."

Mildred said, "Jack was making good money compared to most."

Jack said, "Twice as much as other folks. Of course, that was for a limited time. There were four months of spring and two months of summer. I had the equivalent of a year's wages during that time period, and then I worked for a dollar a day for the rest of the year. Our rent was $6 a month. The Depression really wasn't over until WWII started. Many things were needed for the war effort, including big building projects, which provided jobs for a lot of people, and that got us over the depression. Family was important during this time."

My parents and baby Barbara Jean

Mom and Barbara

The first few years that my parents were married, they attended Zeeland Reformed Church. Dad was working in the hatchery on Sundays, so they didn't get to go much. Then they moved into Zeeland and lived just two houses down from Dad's parents, Henry and Gertrude Van Hoven, for a short time. After that they moved to a house on the next street over, and their daughter, Barbara Jean Van Hoven, was born on August 20, 1934.

Dad said, "When your mom was in labor, my mother came to the house to help. I was giving Mildred the anesthesia. The doctor said, 'not too much,' and my mother said, 'give her some more.' I'd put a mask over her face and sprinkle chloroform on the mask. It was a long labor; well, I suppose it wasn't longer than most, but the doctor was there all night. While he was there, he ate my whole watermelon. I was a little disgusted with him."

Mildred said, "Another thing I remember about that summer is that it was terribly hot, and the night Barb was born it turned cold. The heating system didn't work in the house, and Grandma was concerned because of the baby."

Jack added, "There was hot water heat in that house, but we didn't have it hooked up yet."

Barbara was the first grandchild on both sides of the family, so I think she was a little spoiled.

The next year, in 1935, the family moved to Alto, and Jack got a job at a store. He said, "It was a hatchery and a store. The job was to run the incubators and cut meat for customers. I needed to learn the skill of cutting meat to get the job, so I approached the owner, Andy Vander Plug, and asked how long it would take to learn to cut meat. He said, 'The average time is three years.'

Back row: Richard, Gertrude and Jack
Front Row: Mildred (pregnant with Barb), 8-year-old Donald Van Hoven and Irene

"I said, 'Well, I have to know how in six weeks.' I offered to go to work for Andy for no pay, and that got me the job, but I did get paid after the first week. We did not have a car then, but Andy let us use his big car whenever we needed to. It was a very good place to work. We got our groceries and other things free after that. I cut all the meat in that shop, including bacon and hams, but one particular lady wouldn't have me do it because she only trusted Andy.

Mildred said, "In 1936 we had a lot more snow than I ever remembered having before."

Jack said, "Yes, that was the year of the big storm. The snow was so deep, they couldn't get the snowplows through. They put one snowplow after another down the roads until they were stuck, and then they tried to push them through the roads with not very much success. The fact of the matter is that they did not get many roads plowed. To deliver groceries, I drove down two roads that only had one lane.

I also had a very important trip to make—Mildred was pregnant and would soon have our second baby. We needed a nurse at our home, and when it was time for the delivery I was to get our nurse, Gladius Burr, from Ensley Center. Driving there was like driving through tunnels of snow. I was afraid because I was driving through all this whirling snow and I couldn't see very well. The only reason that I could get to the Burr home was because they were having a funeral there. When I arrived, I climbed up on the banks of snow, and when I got to the telephone poles I walked through the wires, which came up to my hips and knees. Finally, I had to duck down to get beneath the crosspieces, but I did make it to the house. Gladius got her luggage, and we made our way back."

Gladius wasn't really a nurse, she just came to help. She came to Jack and Mildred's house in the early part of February, but Dick wasn't born until the 11th of March. Mildred said, "Gladius had to stay so long, and I don't think she enjoyed it. She got homesick really."

Jack said, "Much of that time the roads were not open, but 15 men cleared the road for our baby and for a man on our road who had pneumonia. They dug the whole road out so the doctor could get there."

Because Mildred was so overdue, the doctor had been about ready to induce the labor process, but finally Mildred went into labor on her own. The road was clear for the doctor to get to the house. Jack helped with this birth, as he had with Barb's. All went well, and Richard Glen Van Hoven was born 4 weeks late, on March 12, 1936.

Dick, Mom and Barb　　**Dick**　　**Dick, Mom and Barb**

Donald and Mother Gertrude Dena　　**Irene, Mother Gertrude Dena, and Gertrude**　　**Dick, Grandmother Van Hoven and Barb**

In 1938 the family of four moved to the Sunfield Farm, which was owned by my father's uncle. Although my parents and siblings had their own bedrooms, parts of the house were shared with Dad's aunt and uncle. While living there, Jack helped his uncle on the farm and also worked at the hatchery.

Jack said, "We lived in a little house on the corner, a very small house. Mildred and another woman helped me with the hatchery business, which wasn't doing well. We hit a year when hatching was very poor, and I spent most of my time building equipment to raise the chicks that we couldn't sell. It was all a very bad deal. The fellow who owned the hatchery was the county clerk, and he was arrested for embezzlement while I was there. I was investigated too a little bit, but of course I had

Sunfield Chicken Farm, 1938, Owned by Jacob Van Hovens uncle. Jacob (Jack) worked for him and their families shared the house. All the buildings were surrounded by Hollyhocks.

nothing to do with that. During that time, every two weeks I drove to the doctor in Grand Rapids because of ulcers. This was for a very long stretch of time. Then I heard of this brand spanking new thing called artificial breeding and I looked into it.

"Although I was saved then," said Jack, "it was one of the worst times in my life. I was really afraid to work in the hatchery because it just seemed to me that Satan met me at the door. I could hardly enter, and I spent every night in misery. I went over and over in my mind about what kind of mistake I had made…well, you know, you get over that by just giving that to the Lord. I don't have the slightest idea what caused it, I just remember the awfulness of it. Things like that, you never want to share. Everybody goes through a period of doubting. I remember Pastor Bob saying, 'Be thankful for your doubts, the unsaved have no doubts.'"

Mildred and Barb went to church in Sunfield when they could. No matter where the Van Hovens were living, family was important, and get-togethers common. Sometimes people just dropped in, and sometimes there were planned events to celebrate a birthday or other occasions. Because Jack and Mildred's children were the first grandchildren and great-grandchildren in the family, they were special. The family visited Grandma and Grandpa Van Hoven a lot. They took time to get together to have pictures taken of the four generations of the men and the women:

In 1938, Jack and Mildred's next move was from Sunfield to the Naps Poultry Farm, which was the second-largest poultry farm in the state of Michigan. Jack was brought in to clean up the broiler house. Broilers are chickens that are raised for their meat, and Naps Poultry Farm was having a difficult time raising their broilers; they got sick, and although they did not die immediately, their growth was stunted. Jack also operated the entire farm with some other young men.

Left to right: Ryntje "Irene" (Wentzel) Van Hoven, Gertrude (Van Loo) Van Hoven, Barbara Jean Van Hoven, and Mildred (Cook) Van Hoven

Left to right: Jacob Van Hoven, Henry Van Hoven, Richard Glen Van Hoven, and Jack Van Hoven

Jack Van Hoven

Barb and Dick

Barb and Dick playing with Aunt Gertrude at a Lake Michigan beach.

Jack continued the story: "We all lived there for a year because we had a profit-sharing company, but there was no profit. So we went back to Zeeland, absolutely broke. We lived with my parents for a while and then we moved to an upstairs apartment on the north side of Zeeland. I had no work for a month.

Jack had not forgotten about artificial breeding. In March of 1939 he went for a 3-day training course, and by the first of November he was in business. The family moved to Uncle Mart's farm.

"Before we moved there," said Jack, "I had talked to Uncle Mart about artificial breeding, but he said that no one would ever pay $5 for that. It took from March to November to get 16 farmers to agree to breed at least one cow. We had our first bull out there at Uncle Mart's. People thought the cows would have sickly calves and that it would never work. It was a big step."

"Barb started school while we lived at Uncle Mart's," said Mildred. "She had to walk a half-mile down a very busy road to get there. I remember real plain, that first morning, when she stepped off, just as confidently as can be. She met with some older neighbor kids along the way, but she started by herself. We lived with Uncle Mart for six months or so, and then we moved to the northern outskirts of Zeeland."

I asked my sister Barb what she remembered about her childhood. She said, "The earliest memory I have was when I had whooping cough. I got it first, but I remember my little brother, Dick, who couldn't even walk yet, sitting on his blanket coughing his little head off. When I was very little, about four I think, the house we lived in had a bay window with a window seat. I loved to play on that window seat with my dolls and a tiny white china tea set. To this day, I love tiny white tea sets. I've collected one small dollhouse-sized set, and two little girl-sized sets."

Great-Grandma Ryntje "Gertrude" Wentzel Van Hoven passed away on October 26, 1939 at the age of 76, and was buried in Zeeland Cemetery.

Jack said, "In the first 7 or 8 years of our marriage we lived in 7 or 8 different houses. In 1940 we rented a house and a barn near Zeeland, where we lived for two years. I became more involved in the artificial breeding business. In those days, I worked at the hatchery at night and bred cows during the day. We had four bulls, and there were other bulls in the neighborhood. Once, someone called the police because a bull was so loud that it was heard way into Zeeland. I remember chasing bulls when they would get out. I found one of them three-quarters-of-a-mile from home..

The artificial breeding business just kept growing, and Jack needed more room for his bulls. He also needed a farm of his own so he could raise hay and corn. In 1942 Jack and Mildred found a farm with 50 acres on Baldwin Street, about 1½ miles from downtown Jenison, and they paid $3,500 for it. At this time Barb was in second grade, and Dick was in kindergarten. The property had a big hole in front where a house had burned down, and the hole had become a neighborhood dump. But there was a good little cement building with a barn, and Jack built a small house that cost him $750.

The house was 20 feet by 28 feet, built completely with cement blocks. Mom and Dad covered most of the inside walls with Solidtex (prefabricated plasterboards) except for the big room, which was covered with pine paneling. The rooms were very small, and the bedrooms were not more than 9 feet by 9 feet. Barb and Dick both had little separate rooms that were just large enough for a cot.

After the family moved into their new home in the early spring, there was a big snowstorm. When the snow melted, they looked out into the fields and saw all kinds of flowers looking back at them. They hadn't realized that the property had recently been a tulip, narcissus and daffodil farm. For years, daffodils especially came up no matter what else was planted in those fields.

Mildred and Barb would make up bouquets and sell them door-to-door in Grandville, which became an important part of their income in the early days of the business.

The breeding business grew; they had started with four bulls, and before long they had fifteen. Jack's brother Richard worked for him on a regular basis, and Jack's youngest brother Don helped out with the animals as well.

Jenison itself was a small town. Several homes had been there for a long time, and there was also the Jenison Mill, the Jenison Food Market, and a small gas station on the corner.

Vintage postcard, Jenison, Michigan circa 1950
Photo courtesy Wikimedia Commons

Photo of L. L. Jenison Mill, which was built in 1864. It closed its doors in 1953.

"The mill was operating," said Jack, "and we got our feed there. We didn't trade in the little gas station though; we got our gas and our services done in Grandville."

The Van Hoven farm on Baldwin Street was about two miles from the town of Jenison. There were three small elementary schools in the district, and one of them, Sandy Hill School, was in Jenison, about a half-mile from their home. Sandy Hill School was a one-room schoolhouse, and most of the 35 students walked to school. There were several farms between Jenison and our house, and some new homes had been built on several lots on Baldwin Street. Our house was about a half-mile above the hill, and a few subdivisions with new houses went in below the hill. There were more farms above the hill, but some new houses on lots on that part of Baldwin Street too.

Jack's first connection to Sandy Hill School was when he worked as the janitor. He could do this work in the mornings and late at night. He said, "I think my job was to light the fire in the morning, if I remember right, and so forth. While I was janitor, we had an Airedale dog named Sandy who always came with me to the school at night. One night, I locked the school building and I didn't think about Sandy. He practically chewed the side of the door off to get out, and I had a lot of repair work to do."

World War II began in Europe on September 1, 1939. The United States became involved after Pearl Harbor was attacked on December 1, 1941, shortly before my parents moved to Jenison.

Jack said, "My biggest recollection of those days was that we had to go to the Secretary of State's office to tell them how much gasoline we used. We also had to tell them how many tires we used. This was because gas and rubber were big needs for the war effort. We told them honestly how much we could get along with but I guess other people weren't honest, so we were left short. Getting tires and gasoline stamps was a major thing for our business because we needed them badly. Many other people had all they wanted and more."

Mildred said, "During the war I remember how sugar, butter and gasoline were rationed. We had a couple of cows and I made butter every week for us, as well as for my parents and Jack's parents. When I couldn't buy sugar, I would buy marshmallows and corn syrup to make ice cream. One of my cake recipes called for corn syrup. It was a wonderful applesauce cake, and everyone wanted that recipe."

Mildred remembered the barn fire in 1944. She said, "It was January 6. Barb was home from school that day, Uncle Dick and Jack had gone to the garage in Grandville, and Uncle Don was working for us then too. Don was in the barn, and he came running to the door yelling that the barn was on fire and then ran back to the barn. I grabbed a coat and followed him, but I saw that the flames were coming out of the barn's big door so I went back in the house and called the garage. I told Jack and Dick to come home. Then I called the Grandville Fire Department, but they wouldn't come out. When I asked Jack why, he said, 'Well I guess it was too far away and the snow was too deep.' Then we let the bulls out in the yard."

Jack said, "Don and Mildred had started to lead them out, but when I got there I said we couldn't do that, and we just let them go out on their own to save time. One Jersey bull was caught on a trailer, and by the time we got around to him the trailer was on fire. The rest of the cattle were running all over the place. One bull was hard to handle, and he was out there loose."

Mildred said, "That bull ran down into the basement of that old burned-out house and couldn't go anywhere. Another one was just lying on his side in the roses. After we rounded them all up, we took them next door to Mr. Osterrink's farm. There was nothing in their barn at the time, so we could tie them up there, and they stayed there all through February.

"People gathered, anyone who went by. The wood Jack had used to fix up the barn for the bullpens didn't burn much because it was so green, but the wood for the new part of the house burned, along with the breeding lab. We had stored some things (canned goods and Barb's dollhouse) in the barn temporarily, since we were planning to build onto the house, so these things burned also."

Jack said, "The top of the barn burned off, but the cement portion did not burn. One of the things we lost in the fire was our nice wash machine. It was the middle of the war at that time and supplies were hard to get, but we did the best we could. We put a flat roof on the cement barn, then later we moved a 40' by 60' barn to the property. My brother Dick and I tore down that barn and rebuilt it

Our first Jenison house, with addition, 1942

ourselves, a job that the neighbors said was impossible."

"Jack was president of the PTA at that time," said Mildred, "so people were familiar with us. Our neighbors had a shower for us at the school. and it was a good thing that he walked in the school and saw the preparations before I came in. He steadied me as we entered because I was so surprised. A table was full of all kinds of supplies including lots of canned goods."

"How nice they were," said Jack. "The whole neighborhood gathered around to bring us all the things we had lost in the fire."

As soon as they were able, Jack and Mildred began enlarging the family house into a tri-level. Barb's room became an extension off the living room, and Dick's old room became a larger bathroom. He moved to our parents' bedroom. Downstairs there were two sections: one section had a large entrance to the artificial breeding business, which contained an office and a laboratory. The other half was used for laundry; it also had a shower, a fruit cellar and storage. The upstairs had two large bedrooms. One was our parents' and one was Barb's (and Norma's when she came along). Both bedrooms had walk-in closets.

Richard and Angie (Brummell) Van Hoven

Uncle Dick married Angieline "Angie" Brummel in the early 1940s. Angie was the daughter of John Brummel (1885-1970) and Alice Tanis Brummel (1888-1943). She was a nurse, and they met when Dick was in the hospital. They lived in Zeeland, and Dick continued to work with Jack.

I was born at 7:50 p.m. on June 6, 1945 at St. Mary's Hospital in Grand Rapids. I weighed 8 lbs., 3½ oz. and was 21 inches long. I was the first of my parents' children to be born in a hospital. Because of a flu virus that had been going around, the hospital was very full at that time. My mother's bed was in the hallway. Everyone was eager to get out of the hospital because of the flu. Aunt Angie was a nurse, so when I was three days old, we went to Aunt Angie and Uncle Dick's house in Zeeland. In those days, maternity patients and babies usually stayed in the hospital for a longer time. Before long, Mildred and I joined our family at home. At this time Barb was 10 years old and Dick was 8.

Norma Sue Van Hoven

Barb (holding Norma) and Dick

March 10, 1946 was a very sad day. Mildred was hurried to the hospital, where she gave birth to a baby girl who my parents named Patricia. Sadly, Patricia died several hours later. Jack remembers what a sad time that was. There was no funeral, and he remembers walking to the tiny grave with Pastor Douglas.

On February 27, 1947 Uncle Donald Van Hoven married Sylvia Bos, who was the daughter of Gerrit and Petilda Bos. In 1950 Donald and Sylvia lived in Blendon, where Don was worked in the stockroom at a brass foundry. In 1956 the family was living in Holland. They had three sons: Scott Eric (b.1948), Mark (b. 1950), and Chris (b. 1952).

Donald Van Hoven **Donald and Sylvia (Bos) Van Hoven**

I remember getting to stay overnight at Grandma and Grandpa Van Hoven's house. One of the first things Grandma did was bake bread. She would roll the dough out on the kitchen table, and sometimes I got to help. It smelled and tasted so good!

Grandpa's tiny garden in the backyard was always a wonder to explore. The pretty flowers smelled so good, and there were wonderful things to eat. I loved to look for a good tomato that would be growing up one of the poles. I used to love to play on the stairs that led to the second floor. I would line all my dolls and stuffed toys on the stairs and play school or house. The library at the top of the stairs was great, too. And I remember Grandpa's great big bear hugs!!

My dad and me

I loved spending time with my dad as he worked around the farm. There were big stones alongside the barn that had been pulled out of the fields to make the plowing possible, and my siblings and all my friends had fun climbing all over them and hiding behind them. Some of the stones were quite colorful and pretty. It was fun to climb the hay bales in the barn also. When my brother built his many hidden camps in the hay barn, my little friends and I always tried to find them but we seldom did! My friends and I also looked under boards that were laying around to see if there were any mouse families with their tiny pink babies.

I also remember loving to be in the kitchen, where I got to have "coffee" with Dad and Uncle Dick. Uncle Dick loved to dunk his toast and jam into his coffee. I got to have toast and jam too, and I copied Uncle Dick's habit.

Our family managed to get away at least once a year. For many years, we rented a cottage on Baptist Lake. While there, we also visited my aunt and uncle, who lived near the lake. My cousin Eleanor would come to the lake to play with me.

Barb, Mom, me and Dick, possibly at Maranatha

Dad tries to get Barb into the canoe with Ed

Eleanor (right) and I watch from the shore

In March of 1947, the whole Van Hoven family got together to celebrate Henry and Gertrude Van Hoven's 40th anniversary.

Left to right around the table: Gertrude Van Hoven, Grandpa Henry Van Hoven, Grandma Gertrude Van Hoven, Donald and Sylvia Van Hoven, Richard and Angie Van Hoven, Irene Van Hoven, Barbara Van Hoven, Jack Van Hoven, Richard "Dick" Van Hoven, Norma Van Hoven, and Mildred Van Hoven.

When I was 5 or 6, Dad became interested in race horses. He was caring for mares, whose colts were going to be trained as racehorses. So when the colts were little and in our care, I got to play with them. We would chase each other, and when we got tired we'd take a break. I would pet them and talk to them. It was so much fun and I loved those colts very much, so I was always sorry to see them go on to their next home. At that time, our family went to a lot of sulky races at the fairs.

Danny   **Fury**   **Daisy Mae**

My father liked chickens, and he always went to the fairs to see the show chickens. He even showed chickens himself for a while. For a couple of years we had bantam chickens, which were small and very colorful but very mean. They would chase us kids if we came close to the barn.

He also began raising and breeding basset hounds, and he competed with other basset breeders. He often had a champion trail dog. In fact, so many of his dogs were winners that other breeders did not like to compete when he was in the running. After a while, our father concentrated on artificial breeding and no longer entered competitions. Jack also raised and studied the genetics of mice. Our family was not as thrilled about that, so we did not complain when he gave up that hobby.

My parents were very involved in the church. Mom taught Sunday School to preschoolers, and Dad was the Sunday School Superintendent. I remember when he would lead the singing for the children's department assembly. He loved to sing, and my mother played the piano.

Pastor Douglas, who led Hudsonville Baptist Church, helped Dad grow in his leadership skills. What I remember most was the little song that Pastor Douglas taught, which Dad sang for years even after Pastor Douglas was long gone. Dad even sang it in a Scottish descant, just as Pastor Douglas had:

Cheer up ye saints of God. There is nothing to worry about.
Nothing to make ye feel afraid. Nothing to make ye doubt.
Remember Jesus never fails. So why not trust Him and shout.
You'll be sorry you worried at all tomorrow morning.

I also learned another song, which I still love today:

"Every step I take I take with Jesus, He is always at my side.
Over hills and walking in the valley, He will always be my guide.
Every step I take I take with Jesus. When beset or stormy tried,
He's my strength, He is my hope of glory. In His love I will abide."

Pastor Murfin was the other pastor I remember, and he and my dad became good friends. They were always praying and talking together about what the Lord had done for the church and for both of them. Pastor Murfin encouraged Dad to look into starting a church in Jenison. They remained friends, even after Pastor Murfin moved to another church in Indiana. And Dad did begin a church in Jenison.

Christmas 1950

Standing: Dick Van Hoven, Donald Van Hoven, Gertrude Van Hoven with Norma Van Hoven, Grandma Van Hoven with Scott Van Hoven, Mildred Van Hoven, and Barbara Van Hoven.
Seated: Angie Van Hoven, Sylvia Van Hoven, Irene Van Hoven, Grandpa Van Hoven and Dick Van Hoven.

Norma and Scott

On April 17, 1952, Dad's sister Gertrude Van Hoven and Donald Van Dyke were married. Jack's sister Irene and my sister Barb were bridesmaids. Gertrude and Don lived in Standale, and I loved to visit Aunt Gertrude. They had two children, Kevin and Katherine.

Kevin Van Dyke shared the following about his parents and their family: *A family cousin who was the son of Herman M. Van Dyke (1882-1950) and Jennie Stark Van Dyke (1885-1964) introduced Gertrude and Don. During World War II, Don was stationed in Hawaii and Guam, and*

Gertrude Van Hoven Van Dyke

Gertrude Van Hoven and Donald Van Dyke

Bridesmaids: Niece Barbara Van Hoven (far left) and sister Irene Van Hoven (far right)

he fought in the Pacific. After he returned home he worked as a sheet metal assembler, installing heating ducts, etc. He also attended Michigan State University and graduated as a horticulturist. Don loved to grow plants, but it must not have paid enough because he eventually worked for Grand Rapids Gypsum Company as the quality assurance person for ten years. After that, Don worked as a school teacher until he retired.

Kevin liked to say, "I had my dad for a teacher, but he kicked me out of his class. Having a parent in another position of authority is not always good. You can't do anything right, and you can't do anything wrong. So I went to another class, and everything worked out. He was a good dad."

Gertrude had worked in a grocery store until she married Don. The family were charter members of Standale Reformed Church, and Gertrude and Don attended there as long as they were able.

Kevin said, "The early years of memories with my mom have faded, but my main memory of her was her love for us. I also remember the rheumatoid arthritis that she developed and tried to control over twenty years of her life. She was always in pain, and later the crippling disease put her in a wheelchair. She made the best of it and took pain medication every day. Mom had surgeries on her elbows and she tried experimental treatments. You never heard her complain. She was a good mom."

Gertrude and Don's family spent many Sunday afternoons at Grandpa Henry and Irene's house. Kevin remembers how Grandpa Van Hoven would listen to or watch the Detroit Tigers after dinner. He also remembers Grandpa's prolific garden.

When Grandpa was getting older Kevin remembered their family, mostly his dad, helping Grandpa prepare the garden for planting. Kevin also remembers taking lots of cigar boxes home from Grandpa's to use for storage. Grandpa had worked rolling cigars in his early life, and he did smoke cigars occasionally.

When Kevin received his driver's license, he got Grandpa Henry's '55 Chevy. Kevin says, "It was very well used, rusted around the headlights and such. But it ran, and I learned how to repair a car. God was watching out for me, because I could have died a few times driving the Chevy. I was thankful to God and to Grandpa for that car."

Kevin also reported, "It is my understanding that Grandpa liked to fish in Lake Michigan off the pier. I was supposed to go fishing with him, but I never got the opportunity. He was getting older by then. One thing I have of his is his fishing knife with a serrated edge.

"We were close to Irene (Ikie). Being that my mother Gertrude and Irene were the girls in the family, they stuck together, and we saw Irene the most. We knew that Mother played the guitar, and she and Irene sang together and even made some records. My sister Kathe has the guitar and some of the records.

"Irene never married. She took care of Grandpa and worked at Grand Rapids Supply Co. until she retired. It is my understanding that she could have married a farmer in the Zeeland area but she decided that she did not want to be a farmer's wife, so she passed it up.

"We also went to mom's brother, Uncle Dick, and Aunt Angie's house for dinner. Uncle Dick would make the dinner (Angie did not like to cook) and I thought it was always good. Angie and us kids would clean up and do the dishes.

"At about the time Dick could not get upstairs anymore, they made a bedroom/sitting room downstairs. That is where we would socialize; just talk, no TV, no radio. One of my memories of that time was that it seemed like every time they got together, Uncle Dick would joke with my dad about him being a school teacher at Grandville Junior High School. He would joke that teachers made too much money. It was always in fun and we would all laugh. Dad was a good sport."

Kevin and Ricky's wedding day
Standing: Kathe, Donald, Kevin and Ricky Van Dyke
Seated in wheelchair: Gertrude Van Dyke

Grandma Gertrude Van Hoven passed away on October 22, 1952 at the age 63. I remember that at her funeral I was sitting near the front with my parents and Barb and Dick. I was seven years old, and had never gone to a funeral before. I remember hearing lots of nice things being said about Grandma, for example that she was a wonderful person and a wonderful grandma. I enjoyed listening until all of a sudden I saw that everyone seemed to be crying. I looked at my sister and she was crying, and then I started to cry too. I missed Grandma, but I still went to her house to visit, even to stay overnight, because Irene and Grandpa were still there.

At night, sometimes I would come and sit by my dad and he would recite his favorite poems for me. One poem, *The Touch of the Master's Hand*, meant so much to me that I learned to recite it, too.

The Touch of the Master's Hand
by Myra Brooks Welch (1877-1959)

'Twas battered and scarred, and the auctioneer thought it sacredly worth his while
To waste much time on the old violin, but held it up with a smile;
"What am I bidden, good folks," he cried, "Who'll start the bidding for me?
A dollar, dollar"; then "Two! Only two? Two dollars, and who'll make it three?

Three dollars, once; three dollars twice; Going for three....." But no,
From the room, far back, a gray-haired man came forward and picked up the bow;
Then, wiping the dust from the old violin, and tightening the loosened strings
He played a melody pure and sweet as a caroling angel sings.

The music ceased, and the auctioneer, with a voice that was quiet and low,
Said: "Now what am I bid for the old violin?"
And he held it up with the bow.
"A thousand dollars, and who'll make it two? Two thousand! And who'll make it three?
Three thousand, once, three thousand, twice and going, and gone," said he.
The people cheered, but some of them cried, "We do not quite understand.
What changed its worth." Swift came the reply: "The touch of the master's hand."

And many a man with life out of tune, and battered and scarred with sin,
Is auctioned cheap to the thoughtless crowd, much like the old violin.
A "mess of pottage," a glass of wine; a game – and he travels on.
He is "going once," and "going twice," he's "going" and almost gone.
But the Master comes, and the foolish crowd never can quite understand.
The worth of a soul and the change that is wrought by the touch of the Master's hand.

Another of my dad's favorite poems:

Wit's End Corner
by Antoinette Wilson

Are you standing at "Wit's End Corner," Friend with troubled brow?
Are you thinking of what is before you, And all you are bearing now?
Does all the world seem against you, And you in the battle alone?
Remember – at "Wit's End Corner" Is just where God's power is shown.

Are you standing at "Wit's End Corner" Blinded with wearying pain,
Feeling you cannot endure it, You cannot bear the strain,
Bruised through the constant suffering, Dizzy and dazed, and numb?
Remember – at "Wit's End Corner" Is where Jesus loves to come.

Are you standing at "Wit's End Corner? Your work before you spread,
A mountain of tasks unfinished And pressing on heart and head.
Longing for strength to do it, Stretching our trembling hands?
Remember – at "Wit's End Corner" The Burden-bearer stands.

Are you standing at "Wit's End Corner? Then you're just in the very spot
To learn the wondrous resources of Him who faileth not:
No doubt to a brighter pathway Your footsteps will soon be moved,
But only at "Wit's End Corner" Is the "God who is able" proved.

Barb was an excellent big sister. She was born in 1932 and I was born in 1945, but despite the age difference she always had time for her little sister, even though she was busy with school activities and work. She was specifically helpful when she took care of me while our parents were away. Even after she was married, she had me stay at her house often. And when I married and became a mom too, she helped me out with supplies and tips. We also enjoyed doing things like crafts and going places, for example to Gaither Music events together.

Between Barb's junior and senior years of high school, she went camping at Holland State Park with several of her friends. That is where she met Ed Schild, who was staying there at the same time. It did not take long before they were boyfriend and girlfriend, and Barb brought him home to meet the family. I liked Ed a lot and wanted to marry him too. Ed said that I was not old enough, but when I was old enough he would marry me too.

Barb and Ed **Ed and me**

CHAPTER 9
Jack and Mildred Van Hoven's Children Have Families of Their Own

BARBARA JEAN VAN HOVEN and Edgar Schild were married on November 1, 1952. They first lived in a couple houses in Grand Rapids. On many Sundays their family would come to our house for dinner. When Dad put a separate street on his farmland and sold plots, he gave some land to Barb and Ed and they built a house there.

They had four children: Bruce Edward (b. November 12, 1953); Sharon Kay (b. May 19, 1956); Mary Jo (b. Jan. 21, 1961) and Laura Ann (b. November 6, 1961).

Ed & Barb Schild Family Story (Photos shared by daughters Mary and Laura)

Barb and Ed's Wedding Party

Virginia Cook, a school friend, Marion Schild, Barb & Ed Schild, Lee Schild, Roger ?, Dick Van Hoven, and flower girl Marsha Duby

Ed and Barb at home

Barb with Bruce Edward

Sharon Kay

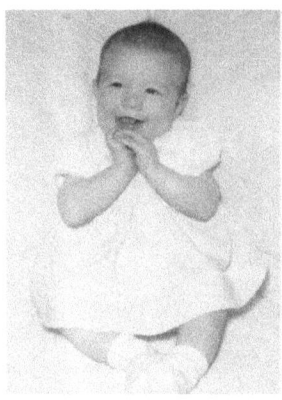
Mary Jo

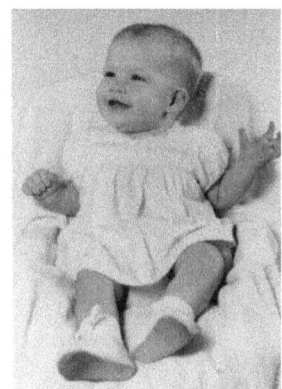
Laura Ann

Barb with Sharon, Ed, and Bruce at Woodward Ave. Baptist Church

Bruce

Bruce, Sharon, Laura and Mary

Mary and Laura

Laura and Mary

As their daughter Laura Schild recalls, "My sister Mary and I got a dollhouse for Christmas in 1966 when we were 5 years old. The story of my love for dollhouses, however, started long before I was even born. When Mom was a girl she started at a new school, and there was a dollhouse in the classroom. She was in love with it, and at home she talked about it constantly. She would talk about how wonderful it was, and that she wished she had one. So Grandpa made her a dollhouse for Christmas, along with all the furniture. As Barb grew up she no longer played with the dollhouse so it was moved out to the barn. Sadly, when the barn burned down, the dollhouse was destroyed. Mom never forgot her beloved childhood dollhouse though, so when she had daughters of her own she passed that love on to us."

Grandpa Jack Van Hoven at Mary's 6th Birthday

Sharon's daughter Naomi and husband Jim Malone and their children, Evelyn and Harleigh

Sharon's son Jeremy and his wife with granddaughter Harleigh, Sharon, grand-daughter Evelyn, and daughter Naomi

When I was ten years old, we moved from the house at the back of the property to a new house that was built closer to the road. When it was under construction, the builder was very friendly to this little girl. He took me around to show me the rooms, and he let Karen and me play in the basement when it was safe to do so. The basement became our playground until the house was ready for us to move in, which was in 1955.

Our new Jenison house, 1955

The house had three bedrooms upstairs; Dick and I each had one, and my parents had the other one. There was also a bedroom in the basement, which was used for visitors. Also in the basement there was one large room, a printing room for dad's business, and two smaller storage rooms. Dad had planned to use Dick's room as an office when Dick left home, so it had a door that opened to the outside, and it certainly made a great office. On the first floor there was a living room, a dining room, a kitchen and a laundry room next to the back door entrance. We had a great attached garage, where we had an extra freezer and plenty of storage.

Dick's Graduation Photo, 1954

Dick and Betty Van Hoven on their wedding day, July 1, 1955

Shortly after we moved in, Dick was married to Elizabeth "Betty" Joan Clossen. Dick and Betty had four children. Janice (b. January 3, 1956); Judy (b. November 23, 1957); Jack (b. March 1, 1959, and James (b. September 11, 1962).

Dick and Betty moved into our old house when they were married. Before long, there was a well-worn path between the houses. Dick worked with Dad, and the lab was still in the basement of the old house.

The well-worn path **Jan and Judy Van Hoven in front of my parents' house.**

Dick and Jan with a Basset hound

Janice, Judy and Jack

James Van Hoven

In 1956, when I was in 6th grade, my good friend Marianne Harwood and I made skirts for ourselves in 4H. On the night of April 3, there was a big 4H fashion show at Hudsonville High School. My folks and I picked up Marianne, and when we arrived at the school my parents went to the gym for the program and Marianne and I went to a classroom to get ready for the show. Suddenly, someone came into the classroom and said that a tornado had been sighted. All the parents were held in the gym, and all of us kids were taken into the hallway, where we were made to sit against the walls. I really didn't know what a tornado was but I was really afraid, and I was worried about my parents. After some time it was decided that we were safe, and we went back into the classroom. The parents were allowed to come and get us kids. I remember looking out the classroom window and seeing how yellow it looked outside.

Our parents were told that the tornado had hit some houses not far from the school, and to be very careful going home. My parents picked up Marianne and me, and we started for home. We were soon turned back, because the tornado had crossed the road we were on, leaving a lot of damage. We ended up taking Chicago Drive all the way back to Jenison, and then we headed up Baldwin toward our house. When we got to the hill about a half-mile from our house, the police were not allowing anyone to go through, and we really began to worry. Would we find our house intact? Dad told the police that our house was up the hill, and they finally let us go toward home. When we arrived, we found that we did still have a house, but there were all kinds of emergency vehicles, sirens blaring, rushing past our house.

Dad dropped Mom and me off at home. He needed to get Marianne home because we knew her parents must be worried. He finally found a road that would take them to her home, and they found that everyone was safe. Marianne's family was so glad to see her. After Dad checked in at home, he drove down Baldwin toward the damaged area to see if he could help. About 20 homes along Baldwin had been damaged, and he found that some of our friends, who did not have a basement, had lost their home. The family

After the tornado we saw the devastating damage.

had all gone into a bathroom in the middle of the house, and this was the only room that survived. Later we learned that a family whose son went to my school not only lost their home, but also their youngest child. All the family members had gone into the basement, and something heavy had fallen on her. After Dad got home, he discovered some damage to the barn, but it was fixable.

When we returned to school after the tornado, the playground looked a lot like the field behind the car that is pictured above. At least there was nothing as big as a car in the field, but there were many pieces of wood and things like tea kettles, etc. We cleaned up the playground, and for the rest of the school year we used these things to play house. Although we were used to having regular fire drills, now we also had tornado and storm drills as well. Sometimes, when bad weather was the forecast, school was cancelled.

When summer came, it was great to get away and go camping at Wilderness State Park. It was quiet, yet kind of wild, and it had become one of our favorite places to go in Michigan. There were several different kinds of animals, and of course we enjoyed Lake Michigan.

In 1956, my parents and some other people began thinking about starting a Baptist Church in Jenison. I remember that my parents, along with Al Faber, began a boys and girls club. They met one night a week in the old Sandy Hill School. So many neighborhood kids began coming that it was divided into two clubs, one night for girls and one night for boys. They played games, had Bible lessons, and memorized verses. Everyone

Dad loved to lie on the beach and listen to the water.

had a beanie cap, and they were given little charms to represent each Scripture verse they learned. They sewed the charms onto their beanies.

Not long after that, Dad began talking to families in Jenison about starting the new church. A couple from Hudsonville who had four kids, Stan and Margaret Van Antwerp, expressed interest in helping. The Van Haitsma family, who lived not far down the street from us, and the Reimersma family, who lived down the hill and had six kids, also joined the group. Finally, the Floras, who lived above the hill, joined us with their four kids.

On October 14, 1956, the first Sunday School was held in a small schoolhouse on the corner of Baldwin and Cottonwood in Jenison. A bus picked up kids in Jenison. On Sept. 8, 1957, the Sunday School moved to Sandy Hill School, at Baldwin and 20th Ave. Then on Oct. 6, 1957, the Christian Fellowship Church held its First Worship Service. The first trustees of the church were Bob Curtis Jr., Paul Helmus, Bill Osborn, Paul Riemersma, Ray VanHaitsma, and Jack Van Hoven.

The church's name was changed to Baldwin Heights Baptist Church in February of 1958, and the Sandy Hill School was purchased. It is said that my father, as the church board president, offered the School Board a dollar for the building, and the school board president, who was also my father, accepted. Of course, both organizations had other board members who were all in agreement.

Sandy Hill School being moved across the fields to its new site as Baldwin Heights Baptist Church

Sandy Hill School after it was moved to its new foundation.

Remodeled and serving as Baldwin Heights Church, April 1958

Pastor Bob Curtis

Grandpa Henry and Grandma Gertrude Dena Van Hoven's 50th anniversary, March 7, 1957

Then the school building was moved to the property that Dad had donated to the church. I remember that day well. Somehow, the jacked-up old school building was pulled across the still-frozen, somewhat muddy fields for about a half-mile until they got across the road from our property. Then they crossed the road and set the school down on a new basement. The first service at the new site was on April 20, 1958.

In September of 1958 the church called its first pastor, Pastor Bob Curtis, Sr. He was married to Doris Curtis, my Hudsonville Baptist Church Sunday School teacher. They were an older white-haired couple, but very active. Mrs. Curtis played the piano for the services and Pastor Bob preached. I remember that when the services were over, Pastor Bob would greet everyone when they left the church. He asked me (and everyone else) several times if we knew Jesus as Savior.

Since the property that Dad had donated to the church was next to our house, it wasn't long before a well-worn path was visible between the two buildings. We often had hymn sings in our basement on Sunday evenings after church, with Al Faber playing the piano and Dad leading the singing. Al could play just about anything, so people would ask for their favorites and Al could usually play them. Our house also hosted Pioneer Girls meetings, and all kinds of other church parties and meetings were held in the basement.

I had taken piano lessons for a while, but while I loved music I did not enjoy playing the piano much. I did, however, love to sing. Everyone thought I had a good voice too, so my parents let me take voice lessons. I loved it, even though the teacher was very professional and tough. I loved singing in a trio all through high school, and doing a lot of solos as well. I sang with the church choir, and whenever we did a cantata I would almost always have a solo. But my favorite cantata was the one at which my dad had a solo, too. He sang "The Longer I Serve Him, the Sweeter He Grows." I get tears even today when I hear that song. Everything it says epitomizes my dad.

"The Longer I Serve Him, the Sweeter He Grows."
by Bill and Gloria Gaither, 1965

Since I started for the kingdom, since my life He controls;
Since I gave my life to Jesus, the longer I serve Him, the sweeter He grows.

Every need He is supplying, plenteous grace He bestows.
Every day my way gets brighter.
The longer I serve Him, the sweeter He grows.

The longer I serve Him, the sweeter He grows.
The more that I love Him, more love He bestows.
Each day is like heaven, my heart overflows.
The longer I serve Him, the sweeter He grows.

In 1960, my good friend Marsha Straatsma was seeing a guy named John Den Boer, who lived in Grand Rapids, but he didn't have his driver's license yet. He told Marsha that his friend, Marv Alkema, could drive, but that she would have to find someone for Marv to date. Marsha asked me if I would be interested, and I agreed. My parents thought I was too young to date, but they gave in as long as we double dated.

Marv and me

Marv and I went on our first date on January 5, 1960, which was Marv's 17th birthday. We didn't do much besides ride around, and then we went to Marsha's house. But that was the beginning of a long relationship. By my 16th birthday in June 1960, Marv and I were going steady, and we dated all through high school. Marsha was my Maid of Honor when Marv and I married.

I did well in high school, graduating with an Honors diploma. There was only one problem: I became engaged to Marv just before senior exams. I tried to study as much as I could, and I made As and Bs on all my exams except for Advanced Math. I got a D and I was mortified, but at least I got a C+ for the semester because I did better in my coursework before the exam.

I was honored to be asked to sing at the Commencement Program. I asked my friend Carol Messer to accompany me on the piano. The song I chose was "I Know Who Holds Tomorrow." That song has always meant a lot to me.

My high school graduation photo, 1963

The commencement began with an Invocation and ended in the Benedictory Prayer. When I sang it was like giving my testimony at graduation. It is so different in public school today, where even prayers are disallowed. I love the story of the valedictorian who sneezed at the end of his speech on purpose and all the classmates said, "God Bless You."

In the summer of 1963 I was the office girl at Michi-Indi Cherith Camp. On the last week of camp I even got to be a counselor when one of the counselor's got sick and had to go home. I continued as counselor at Michi-Indi whenever I could. My sister, Barb Schild started going to camp as a cook.

I worked at Michi-Indi Cherish Camp, in the office and as a counselor.

Marv and I were married on February 14, 1964.

My parents, me and Marv, and Marv's mother Margaret Alkema Martin

Our Wedding Party: Best Man Tom Alkema, Marv and me, and Bridesmaid Marsha Straatsma

Nephew and nieces: Jack and Judy Van Hoven, Sharon Schild, Jan Van Hoven holding Laura Schild and Mary Schild. Two nephews, Bruce Schild and Jim Van Hoven, are not pictured.

Before Marv and I married I worked at Montgomery Wards, but after we married I stayed at home. Our first home was an upstairs apartment at 905 Richmond Street in Grand Rapids. The entrance was at the back of the house, and we had a kitchen, dining room, living room, bedroom and a tiny room over the front porch. Marv had grown up in the northwest side of Grand Rapids, so living there was not strange to him, but to me it was strange as I had never lived in a city. Marv worked at Capital Lumber Company and as the youngest sales person, sometimes he was asked to do things the others didn't want to do. One of his jobs was to close up at night. Before long though, he had regular customers who asked for him because he was so helpful; he knew what they wanted, and where to find it. Before long, sometime yet in 1964, Marv got a job working in Jay Rode's Tool and Die Shop. He did really well, and he also took two years of tool and die training at Grand Rapids Junior College.

Our daughter Amy Sue Alkema was born on September 29, 1964. She weighed 8 lbs. 7 ozs. and was 21" long.

Marv was a very involved daddy.

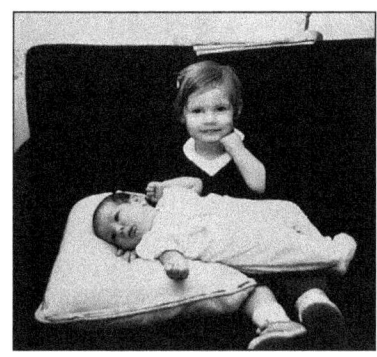 

Barbara Joy Alkema was born on November 5, 1966. She weighed 9 lbs. and 3 oz. and was 20½ inches long. Amy was very happy to have a baby sister. We were glad to have two girls so close in age. Our house was now full.

CHAPTER 10
Through the Years: 1966-1983

CHRISTMAS 1966 was special because Grandpa Cook, my grandfather on my mother's side, was there. When Amy saw him coming in with his cane, she pointed and said, "Candy cane." Year after year, as the family grew, we all got together for Christmas.

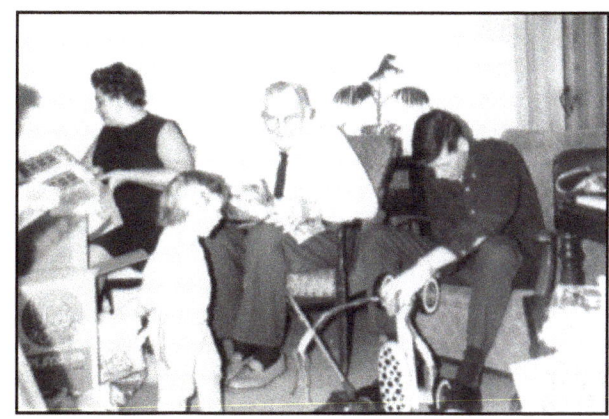

Barb Schild, Amy Alkema, Grandpa George Cook, and Marv Alkema

This collage was presented to my father on his 58th birthday, 1967.

99

On June 26, 1970, Grandpa Henry Van Hoven passed away. I missed him, just like I missed my grandma. Whenever I come into Zeeland, I go past their house on Maple Street. I always have good memories about our times there.

In the summer of 1969, my sister Barb and I both worked at Pioneer Girls Michi-Indi Camp Cherith. I was the counselor for junior high girls and Barb cooked all the meals.

Barb Schild, cook

I had a lot of fun with the junior high girls

My parents and the cousins celebrated Barbie's 3rd birthday in 1969.

Van Hoven Christmas 1971: Grandma Mildred, Sharon and Laurie Schild, and Amy Alkema

My dad's birthday, March 1973: Barbie, the Schilds' puppy, Dad and Mom

My parents' 40th Anniversary, August 25, 1973

From left: Mildred & Jack, Marv, Ed, Gertrude & Don Van Dyke, Richard and Angie Van Hoven, and Irene. Barb Schild is in the kitchen and I am taking the picture.

The "big kids": from left, Kathy and Kevin Van Dyke, Jack Van Hoven, Sharon and Bruce Schild, Judy and Janice Van Hoven

The "little kids": from left, Amy Alkema, Laurie Schild, Jim Van Hoven and Barbara Alkema; Mary Schild is hiding.

Van Hoven Christmas, 1974

Almost ready for dinner.

Barbie at the tree with Ed Schild

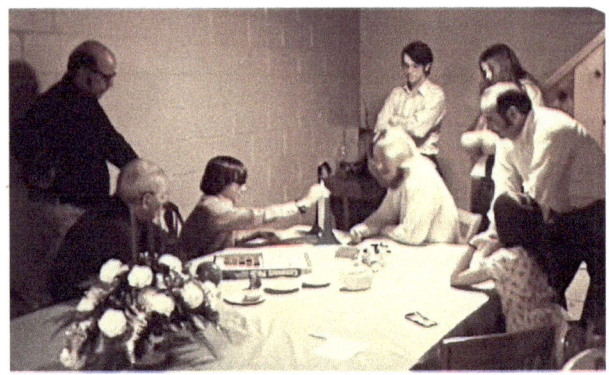
Fun and games: Ed Schild, Grandpa Jack Van Hoven, Jim Van Hoven. Bruce Schild, Bob Gillett, Mary Schild, Dick Van Hoven, & Barbie Alkema

Music was always important to our family. In this photo, my parents' grandchildren make music together: Bruce and Sharon Schild, Jan and Judy Van Hoven.

For some time, Michi-Indi Camp Cherith had rented campgrounds every year. Dad was on the Camp Board when they started looking for campgrounds to purchase. It took a while, but finally the day had come. Michi-Indi Camp Cherith purchased a new campground on a 360-acre site between Sand Lake and Howard City in 1975. A dam was put in to provide a 13-acre lake, which was named Waltman Lake. When Mr. Waltman had visited Israel he brought back some water from Brook Cherith, and in the summer when the camp was dedicated, he poured the water into Waltman Lake.

Brook Cherith Camp was dedicated in the summer of 1975. Waltman Lake was a great fishing spot.

My sister Barb had been the cook at Michi-Indi Camp Cherith, and when Brook Cherith Camp opened she was the head cook. It was a real challenge, especially on rainy days— the kitchen was in a trailer and the dining hall was in a pole barn. It was difficult to bring the meals to the barn without the food getting wet. When we got a new lodge with a dining hall and kitchen, Barb's job became much easier.

Van Hoven Christmas, 1975

November 1, 1976 was Barb and Ed's 25th anniversary

Van Hoven Christmas 1973: From upper left: Dick Van Hoven, Laura Schild, Ed & Barb Schild, Norma Alkema, Barbara Alkema, Amy Alkema, Grandpa Jack Van Hoven, standing, Grandma Mildred Van Hoven

Van Hoven Christmas, 1976

Left side: Bob & Jan Gillett, Jack Van Hoven, Judy Van Hoven, Dick and Betty Van Hoven, Jim Van Hoven
End of table: Norma Alkema
Right side of table from back: Amy and Barb Alkema, Barb & Ed Schild, John & Sharon Monasmith, ?
With their backs to the camera from left: Bruce Schild, Jack & Mildred Van Hoven

From left: Dad, Betty & Dick Van Hoven, and Mom

Van Hoven Christmas, 1977

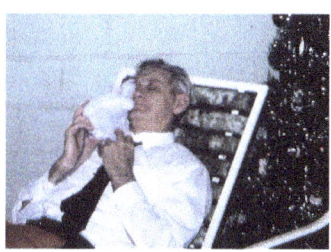

Dad enjoys his gift of a stuffed rabbit.

My parents, Christmas 1977

The Barb Van Hoven Schild family

Back: Barb and Ed Schild, John and Sharon Monasmith
Front: Bruce, Mary and Laurie Schild

The kids who still live at home still get stockings from Grandma Mildred.

The Richard Van Hoven Family

Back: Bob Gillett, Jack and Dick Van Hoven
Middle: seated: Jan Gillet and Betty Van Hoven
Front: Jim and Judy Van Hoven

"The Blizzard of '78" was a memorable event. I remember being so worried about getting out the bulletin for church for the coming Sunday. Some roads were one-lane because the plows could not keep up, and it seemed that when a plow went through, the lanes drifted over immediately.

Someone dropped me off close to church, but I had to climb over many drifts to get into church. I got the information for the bulletin so I could work on it at home. Then before Sunday church was canceled because the blizzard wouldn't stop.

Ed Schild at their house on Mellowood Dr., Jenison

Van Hoven Christmas, 1979

Mom, Janice (Van Hoven) Gillett, Betty and Dick Van Hoven, and Judy (Van Hoven) Pruim and Chuck

My dad raised chickens and showed them at the fair, so he was surprised with the gift of a chicken.

Building snowmen with the cousins in 1980: Barb, Kathy Stapley, Amy, Doug Stapley, and Ken Alkema in front

Barb and the girls' snowmen

Brook Cherith Camp Lodge Dedication, 1981

Esther, Nora Sullivan (BJ), Barb Schild (Bobby), Camp Director (Jay), and Marilyn Mills (Scooter)

Van Hoven Christmas, 1982

Nativity Scriptures and singing carols once again

In forefront left to right: Amy, Ruth Alkema, and Laura Schild and Ed Schild

Mom and Dad's 50th Anniversary, August 25, 1983

Children: standing left to right, Dick and Betty Van Hoven, Dad and Mom, Barb and Ed Schild, and Norma and Marv Alkema

Grandchildren: Standing, Laura Schild, Barb, Sharon Schild Monasmith, Mary Schild Oosterheert, Bruce Schild, Judy Van Hoven Pruim, Jim Van Hoven.
Seated, Amy, Dad and Mom, and Janice Van Hoven Gillett

25th Anniversary, Baldwin St. Baptist Church, October 1982

My dad welcomed guests and gave a brief history of Baldwin Heights Baptist Church.

The original trio: Marge Stevens, me and Marsha Norton

Charter Members

Back row: Dick Van Hoven, Dad, Joyce and Paul, and Jeanette and Ray Van Haitsma; Middle row: Betty Van Hoven, Mom, Margaret Van Antwerp, ? & ?; Front: Stan Van Antwerp

My parents visit with Dad's mentor, Pastor Robert Murfin, and his wife.

Pastor Steve Donohue and family

Pastor Jim and Jan Winn, and Kim

Youth pastor Dan Morrell and family

Pianist Al Faber and his wife, Jane

CHAPTER 11
A New Generation and Many Goodbyes

Van Hoven Christmas, 1984: Amy, my dad, Bob Gillett, Jack Van Hoven, and my parents' two little great-granddaughters

Van Hoven Christmas 1985

In 1985 Sharon and John Monasmith adopted their daughter, Rachel.

Mom is holding Sharon and John's daughters, Naomi and Rachel

Dad wore wooden shoes for farm work as a child, and on his own farm when he was an adult.

Grandpa likes his toys, too!

In 1986 we celebrated my Dad's 77th birthday at our house in Grandville. From left: Dad, Bob Osterheert, Bob and Jan Gillett, and Judy Pruim

BARB AND NATE'S DAUGHTER, Rebecca Joy Sheler, was born on February 19, 1987. As we walked down the hospital hallway, I could feel my heart beating in anticipation of greeting our first-born grandchild. I pushed on room 247's heavy door and it grudgingly opened, removing the last barrier. I smiled at the sight of Mom, Dad, and baby settled on the bed together. As my eyes met the eyes of my daughter and son-in-law, I could feel their joy and pride.

I bent down to offer a hug and put my face into my daughter's smooth hair. Then all my attention was focused on the bundle in her arms. Barb held Rebecca out and placed her in my arms. Rebecca felt so incredibly light and tiny, a soft little ball wrapped up in her blanket. She fit so perfectly into the crook of my arm and the place reserved in my heart. "Welcome, Rebecca Joy Sheler, I will love you forever."

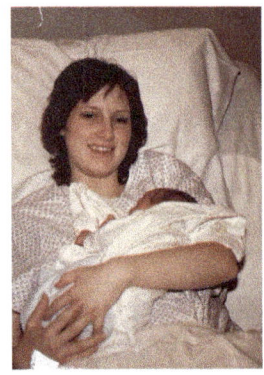 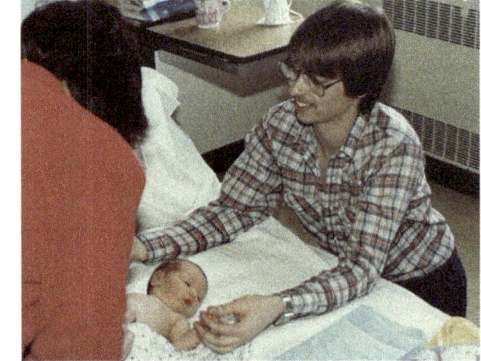 

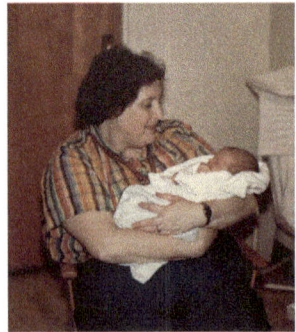 

We were thrilled to welcome Amy's daughter, our second granddaughter, Onnolee Grace Lynch, on April 28, 1987. We were in Tennessee to meet Onnolee that week, and it was Mother's Day. Onnolee, at 9 days old, was the youngest baby at church that Sunday. Amy got a corsage.

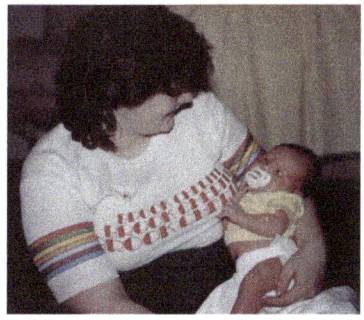
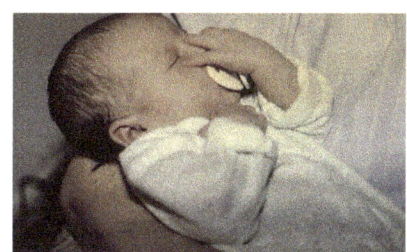

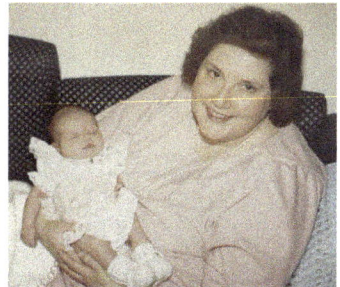
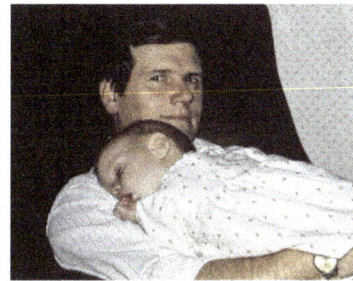

Onnolee and Becca

We celebrated Dad's 79th birthday in March 1988 at Dick and Betty Van Hoven's home in Ensley Center.

Dad is surrounded by his great-grandchildren. From left: Mom, Seth Van Hoven, Holly Oosterheert (kissing Dad who is holding Jordan Van Hoven and Onnolee, Stephanie Gillett, Jeremy and Rachel Monasmith, Cassandra Pruim, Naomi Monasmith, Becca (in highchair) and Allison Gillett. Not pictured: Andrew Gillett and Megan Pruim. (Jacob Sheler was not born yet.)

;Mom and Dad moved from Jenison to Ensley Center, where they built a new house on Mom's parents' old home property. We had Christmas in their new house and enjoyed dinner, Christmas Scripture and carols.

On September 15, 1988, Dad's brother, Donald Van Hoven, passed away at the age of 63. Donald was the youngest of the siblings, but the first one to pass away. He left behind his wife Sylvia and three sons, Scott, Chris and Mark.

On October 30, 1988, Dad's brother Richard Van Hoven, passed away at the age of 79. Richard had worked with Dad for many years, and later he helped his wife Angie when she began running her own nursing home. Richard was crippled from the polio he'd had as a child, and was homebound before his death.

To commemorate our 25th anniversary on February 14, 1989, Marv and I renewed our vows at church and our daughter Barb sang our wedding song. Then we had an open house at our new home in Jenison.

Our 25th anniversary

Marsha (Straatsma) Norton (far left) and Tom Alkema (far right) were in our wedding party.

Becca puts on a show

Gerda and John Den Boer

Dad with Marge and Dave Stevens

Dad had been saying that he was going to retire for a long time. Slowly, he turned General Genetics over to Dick Van Hoven, who now lived next door to Jack near Ensley. It was hard for him, but he know it was for the best.

Jack Van Hoven's Retirement Party, 1989

Dad talks to a friend

Mom makes the introductions: Don Van Dyke, Irene Van Hoven, Angie Van Hoven, Mom, unknown friend, and Stena Gort

Jacob Dean Scheler was born on December 10, 1989. He weighed 7 lbs., 12 oz., and was 21 1/2 inches long.

Dad holds his namesake.

  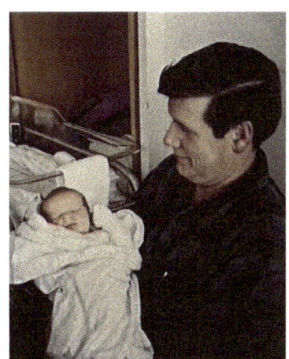

Becca is a proud big sister, and Marv and I are thrilled to welcome a grandson.

On February 10, 1990, Dad's sister Gertrude Van Dyke passed away at the age of 77. Gertrude had been a bookkeeper in retail grocery before she married, after which she became a stay-at-home mom. She had very bad arthritis and was in a wheelchair a lot in later life. She left behind her husband Don and two children, Kathe and Kevin.

Mom's 80th birthday, October 9, 1991

Van Hoven Christmas, 1991

Four generations: Back row, Jack Van Hoven holding Jordon and Richard "Dick" Van Hoven; Front row: Seth standing by Great-Grandpa Jack

Presents for all is a happy time.

Singing and Bible reading of the Christmas story

We celebrated my parents' 60th anniversary on August 25, 1992. A newspaper account read, *"A 60th Anniversary will be observed on Aug. 25 by Jack and Mildred (Cook) Van Hoven of Sand Lake, formerly of Jenison. The occasion will be celebrated with a family gathering. The Van Hovens' children are Richard and Betty Van Hoven, Ed and Barb Schild, and Marv and Norma Alkema. They have 10 grandchildren and 14 great-grandchildren.*

Dad and Mom with Bob Gillett   **Barb serves the cake.**

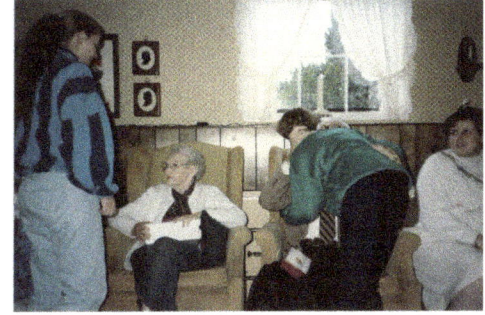

Allison Gillett, Grandma and Grandpa Van Hoven, another grandchild and Barb   **Dad and Mom with Ruth and Jim Van Hoven**

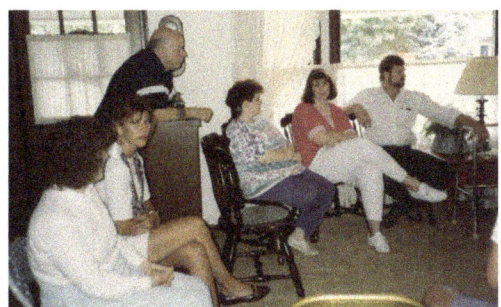

Left to right: Ruth and Beth Van Hoven, Ed Schild, Amy Alkema, and Mary and Bob Oosterheert   **Laura Schild with Dad and Mom**

Mildred Van Hoven's 81st Birthday, October 9, 1992

Barb Schild shows the cake; Jim Van Hoven is to her left. Seated on the couch: Becca Sheler, Onnolee Lynch, Mom, Allison Gillett, Cassie Prium, and Jordon and Beth Van Hoven

Van Hoven Christmas 1992

Becca and Dad   **Dad, Jacob, Nate, Becca and Onnolee**

In 1994 Don and Sylvia Van Hoven's son Scott, my first cousin on the Van Hoven side of the family, passed away at about 46 years old.

In 1994 Barb and Nate's family moved to Jenison. Dad, Mom and Barb were among the visitors.

Van Hoven Christmas, 1995

Still Singing Christmas Carols and Reading Nativity Scriptures Together: John and Sharon Monasmith, Dad and Mom; Great-Grandchildren Naomi and Rachel Monasmith, Onnolee and Becca

By 1996 Mom's Alzheimer's had gotten worse, and both she and dad moved to a nursing home (now American Homes in Jenison). At this time Dad was in one home and mom was in another that specialized in Alzheimer's patients.

Mom at her home at Oakcrest Critical Care

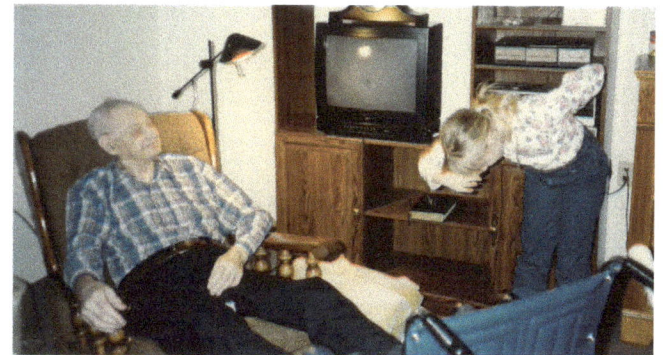

Becca performs her part in her school program for Dad at his home in Oakcrest.

A newspaper article was written in 1997, titled *"Dairyman Honored"*, and it reads as follows: *"Dairyman and businessman Jack VanHoven, of Jenison, (in photo, seated) was honored Aug. 4 by Michigan State University for contributions in his name to the Michigan Dairy Memorial Scholarship Foundation. The foundation awards scholarships to students majoring in food science and human nutrition or animal science, with an emphasis in dairy production and processing. A plaque and picture of Van Hoven will be permanently installed in Anthony Hall at MSU. VanHoven, 89, currently resides at*

Oak Crest Manor. He is the founder of the Zeeland Artificial Breeding Association, and pioneered several innovative techniques in artificial breeding of dairy and beef cattle. His company is called General Genetics, Inc. He also served as president of the Jenison Board of Education, was active in the Gideons, and his church. With VanHoven in the photo are Larry Haywood, of Hastings (left); and Remus Rigg, of Coldwater (right), who initiated fundraising for the scholarships fund in honor of VanHoven's contributions to the dairy industry in Michigan."

On January 3, 1998, my mother, Mildred Van Hoven, passed away at the age of 86. It was a difficult way to start the year. Mom had had Alzheimer's for several years before she went home to heaven. At the end, Mom did not know any of us, so I had lost her before 1998 in many ways. But even when she did not recognize us, I could still talk to her about birds and animals, which she loved. I could show her magazines and still tell her the story of my life. She remained sweet and kind to the end, and she passed away suddenly of heart failure.

When I think of my mom, I think of a very quiet, gentle, and kind woman. As a wife and mother, she rose early to take care of the needs of her family. She made her own bread, butter, and jam; for years she kept a flower garden and a vegetable garden, and she canned the vegetables so we could enjoy them any time of year. The customers at Rainbow Grill enjoyed her pies, which were the best in the world.

Mom sewed most of my clothes when I was little, and later she always made beautiful things, like the lovely patchwork pillows and sweaters for her grandchildren. When I was little, she would give me her empty thread spools to play with, which I made into families, and when I was older she taught me to sew.

Our mother was supportive of Dad in all his endeavors. As the bookkeeper for his business, she made entries in one ledger with her right hand and used her left hand to make entries in another ledger. I had not even noticed that she was ambidextrous until my left-handed boyfriend, Marv, noted that Mom was using her left hand to peel the potatoes when he came over for supper one night. Minutes later, he walked past again and noticed that she was peeling with her right hand. Then one night as she was doing my dad's bookkeeping, I showed Marv that she was again using both hands. It proved his observation, and from then on we noticed it more and more.

I remember my mom to be a good teacher and a great lover of little children. She was always ready to babysit Amy and Barb at our house, or at her house in Jenison. For many, many years she worked with nursery-aged children at church. She cared so much for others. One time, when our neighbor came running to get away from her alcoholic husband, Mom took her in for as long as she needed to stay.

Mom loved to play the piano and she listened to Christian music on the radio as she worked. She loved the Lord deeply, and I often would see her with her Bible open.

On November 16, 1998 my father Jacob (Jack) Van Hoven passed away. Dad died before I could come to see him at the end because I was in the middle of a MS flare-up. I was very dizzy and could hardly walk. But Pastor Denny Emmons from church would visit Dad, and then stop by to visit me too. When we planned Dad's funeral and had visitation, I was in a wheelchair and had a patch over one eye, but by the time of the funeral I was able to walk again and see much better.

From the time I was a child I adored my father, and I wanted to spend as much time with him as I could. I loved and missed him so much. But as the funeral progressed, I felt the whole room radiate with God's presence; it was like He was picking me up in His arms and saying, "You will be all right, I am with you."

When I think of my dad, I think of an outgoing man who would talk to anyone, and when people came away they always felt better about themselves. He was an idea man. He had started his own business with a new idea and became a success. He took classes and worked hard at becoming a good businessman.

Although he cared a lot about his business, he cared more about people. There were very few people he did not like, or that he didn't want to know better. He was very involved in church, especially Sunday School at Hudsonville Baptist Church. When he wanted to reach people in Jenison, he and Al Faber started a club program for kids that grew and grew. He and several others began Baldwin Heights Baptist Church in Jenison in 1957. Dad was gone a lot with his business and church work, and I was kind of jealous of the time and attention other kids got from him. He was always talking about the interesting people he had met.

Dad loved to sing and he led the singing in church, but everyone's favorite times were when my parents had a hymn sing in their basement; Dad led the singing, and Al Faber played the piano. What joyful fellowship.

It was clear that my dad had three loves: the Lord, our mom, and the family. When we kids got married we were very much on our own, but he was always willing to give us advice if we asked. The advice was always good. Dad loved his children and grandchildren and was a praying man. I know he prayed for his 10 grandchildren every day.

Dad was so loving and caring for Mom when she got Alzheimer's, and it broke his heart. When he was confined to the nursing home, I became his librarian. That was such a joy because I got to bring him new books most every week and spend time talking with him. He often talked about the Lord and when he went home to glory he was ready to go.

I wasn't ready to loss either of my parents, but their love and lives are never far from me. They have been in heaven now for 27 years, and I love them dearly and miss them still.

Because of my MS, I left my position as Women's Ministry Director at church. Sadly, I also had to leave my job at Lutheran Child and Family Services. I never knew when I would be unwell, and my clients needed someone who could always be there. It was also necessary for me to be available to testify in court in important cases, and that was not always possible anymore. I did stay on the board of Brook Cherith Camp.

Marv and I wondered how MS would change our lives, because we loved to travel so much and do lots of outdoor things. But the Lord was so good, and He heard my cry. He held me in His hand and protected me under the shadow of His wings. Psalm 57:1: *"In the shadow of Your wings I will make my refuge, until these calamities have passed by."*

My sister Barb's favorite verses became very meaningful to me: Philemon. 4: 6,7: *"Be anxious for nothing, but in everything by prayer and supplication, with thanksgiving, let your requests be made known to God; and the peace of God, which surpasses all understanding, will guard your hearts and minds through Christ Jesus."* While I could not do all I wanted to do, God showed me that I could pray, so that is what I did.

In 1999 Jack's sister, Irene Van Hoven, passed away. In 1943 Irene became a member of the Dutch Christian Reformed Church in Zeeland. While she attended Zeeland High School she was in Glee Club. She and Gertrude also played and sang with other friends. Irene worked as a bookkeeper for Refinery Wholesale. She was 87 when she passed away.

On November 4, 2002, Ed Schild passed away. He had suffered greatly with Alzheimer's. Barb cared for him at home for as long as she could, and we visited him there. After he was hospitalized we did not see him, at Barb's request; Ed had become much worse, and Barb didn't want us to see that. He died at the age of 73.

All of the Van Hoven siblings had now passed away. The spouses that were living were Gertrude's husband, Don Van Dyke; Don's wife, Sylvia, and Richard's wife Angie. Angie had always cared about all of us kids and she wanted to have a cousins get-together at her house, which became a special gathering every year.

I remember one special year, when everyone started talking about the Van Hoven history. I had my Van Hoven/Van Loo scrapbook, which I had researched and had just finished in the car, so Marv went out and got it. We all stood around the table and looked at all the pictures, and I told them a lot about the family. It was quite exciting. I know even more now, and this book is the result.

Angie made this happen for all of us. Her walls were covered with her needlework projects. She loved cats, so there were a lot of cat pictures, but I loved her scenery pictures best. I often commented on her winter farm picture and told her that it reminded me of growing up on the farm. She told that she had done that picture because it reminded her of her childhood home. In 2013 Angie said that she wanted me to have that picture. I took it home, and it hangs in our living room; in the winter it has the place of honor over the wood burner. I love it, not only because Angie did the needlework, but because Uncle Dick had made the frame.

On October 12, 2009 Donald Van Dyke passed away. He was 91 years old.

On Nov. 4, 2016 my sister Barbara Schild passed away. In her final years, Barb was unable to take care of herself. She became confused and was unable to keep track of her medications, so she went to live at American House. Marv and I visited her there regularly. We often found Barb's daughter, Mary Oostenheert, visiting her mom. Mary had decorated Barb's room with all her treasured things so beautifully.

Often, when I visited toward the end of Barb's life, she would be listening to a wonderful tape of favorite hymns and other songs that Mary had put together for her. Barb had even been able to make close friends at American House, and these friends missed her when she was gone. Barb, like our mother, was sweet to the end.

From her obituary: *"Barb was 82 years old when she was welcomed into heaven after her long battle with Alzheimer's. She was preceded in death by her parents Jack and Mildred Van Hoven and her loving husband of 50 years, Ed. She is survived by her brother Dick and Betty Van Hoven of Sand Lake, her sister Norma and Marv Alkema of Jenison, her sister-in-law Marian Schild of Jenison, her children Bruce Schild of Holland, Sharon and Alan Fairbanks of Maine, Mary and Bob Oosterheert of Jenison, and Laurie Schild of Georgia. Also surviving are 4 grandchildren (Holly, Jeremy, Naomi, and Rachel) and 4 great grandchildren (Sienna, Ava, Jackson, and Harleigh).*

Ed and Barb Shild

Barb lived most of her life in Jenison where she dedicated her life to serving the Lord by volunteering for her church and for Pioneer Ministries. She loved working in the church nursery. She was well known for her cooking skills and took charge of all the church banquets. She was always ready to prepare and deliver a meal for a church member when they had a death or illness in the family. She was also a "Pioneer Girls" church leader for many years as she loved working with kids. Her love for cooking and her love of the Pioneer Ministry Program led her to also volunteer as the head cook for the Pioneer Summer Camp program, known as Michi-Indi Camp Cherith where she was known to campers as Bobby. From there Barb and her husband Ed were closely involved with opening a new camp in Sand Lake, MI known as Brook Cherith Camp where Ed served on the camp board while Barb served on the Program Committee and continued as head cook for many years, feeding hundreds of hungry campers over the years. She was known by the caring staff at American House for her warm smile and friendly demeanor. She will be dearly missed by all who have known and loved her."

On April 17, 2021 Uncle Dick's wife, my beloved Aunt Angie Van Hoven, passed away at Cook Valley Estates in Grand Rapids. She was 101 years old. Angie was a charter member of Faith Reformed Church in

Zeeland. She graduated from Zeeland High School in 1937, and from Blodgett School of Nursing in 1940. She served in the Army Reserve Nurse Corps in World War II, and then became a visiting nurse. From 1952-1956 she served as the Director of the Visiting Nurse Association in Holland. In 1956 she owned and operated Woodhaven Skilled Nursing Home in Zeeland; this facility, now known as Heritage Nursing Home, is still in operation at the same location. Angie was a highly talented embroiderer and loved to share her art with family and friends. She was a member of the Grand Rapids Chapter of the Embroidery Guild of America and taught classes through the Guild.

Angie Van Hoven

God saw she was getting tired and a cure was not to be,
So He put His arms around her and whispered, "Come with Me."
With tearful eyes we watched her suffer and saw her fade away.
Although we loved her dearly, we could not make her stay.
A golden heart stopped beating, hardworking hands to rest.
God broke our hearts to prove to us He only takes the best.

Author Unknown

Author's Note

I have enjoyed the hours I have worked in researching and writing this book, and working with my editor, Betty Epperly. She has been a great help. I especially want to thank Marv Alkema, my husband of 61 years, for working so well with me and making time for me to use the computer for all that work.

Right at the beginning of my history-gathering journey, my sister, Barb Schild, made all the family pictures available for me to copy, and we shared the history that we each knew about the different relatives. Barb also did the embroidery piece that is featured on the cover of this book as a gift to our parents, Jack and Mildred Van Hoven. Later, her daughter Laura Schild shared a very special family story and Laura and her sister Mary also shared many family photographs. Thank you, Laura and Mary.

I also want to thank my cousin, Kevin VanDyke, the son of my aunt Gertrude Van Hoven Van Dyke and my uncle Donald Van Dyke. He has been a continuing encouragement in this rather long process. Thank you for sharing the great Van Dyke family story. And thanks for the additional stories from your visits with Grandpa Henry and Grandma Gertrude Van Hoven, and Aunt Irene Van Hoven.

The Zeeland Historical Society and the Dekker Huis Museum graciously allowed me to spend many hours in their historical archives, where I discovered newspaper articles and other documents pertaining to our ancestors. I also read the historical information on both the Holland and Zeeland websites, as well as on Wikipedia.

Ancestry.com was the source for much of the ancestry lineage information. To all who read this book, it is my desire that you will find it a joy and a blessing to learn more about those who came before you.

My dear father's Bible is a much-cherished possession

Psalm 119, verses 105, 111 and 112:

"Your word is a lamp unto my feet,
And a light unto my path.
Your testimonies I have taken as a heritage forever,
For they are the rejoicing of my heart.
I have inclined my heart to perform your statutes
Forever, to the very end."

www.ingramcontent.com/pod-product-compliance
Lightning Source LLC
Chambersburg PA
CBHW061126070526
44584CB00033B/4238